A PICTORIAL HISTORY OF BRAILES LOWER BRAILES PART ONE

EDITED BY ALFRED WOODWARD

RECORDING AND LAYOUT BY BARRY KEELEY BLOCKLEY

TYPESETTING BY GILLIAN BRYAN

Published in 2005 by Braywood Publishing
15, Manor Farm Road, Tredington, Shipston-on-Stour,
Warwickshire, CV36 4NZ, England.

ISBN 0-9551388-0

Vale Press Ltd

Printed and bound in England
by Vale Press Ltd, Willersey. 2005

THE EDITOR'S PORTRAIT
By
Barry Keeley

* * * *

Alfred Woodward was born in The Ellen Badger Hospital on 5th September 1921. He was taken a few days later to his home in SHEPESTREETE, LOWER BRAILES (Sheep Street), and at this village he spent the earlier years of his life. Since those earlier years he has had the burning ambition to produce a village history, this he achieved in 1988, writing the book MEMORIES OF BRAILES. He has now commenced, together with RJ Tait and Barry Keeley, a Pictorial History of Brailes in two parts, Lower Brailes - Part One, Upper Brailes - Part Two. He is now looking forward to its completion, which will be almost 84 years since his birth.

EDITOR'S PREFACE

A Pictorial History of Lower Brailes and of Upper Brailes will be published in two parts - Part One Lower Brailes, Part Two Upper Brailes. Culled from old and new photographs, postcards of the earlier periods of the village history, and produced in the style which Mr George Rainbird described as his invention, he believed that a person reading a book should be able to see the object etc. they were reading about on the same or opposite page, aptly named COFFEE TABLE BOOKS, placed on tables for the guests to browse through, a London Publisher retired, who had asked me to catalogue his collection of books, a copy of all the books he had published in his working life. He had revived my flagging interest in wanting to publish a book on the history of my home village of Brailes, this was achieved in 1988, and a visit from a friend and old work colleague has brought about my second book being prepared for publication, still some work to do.

We have formed a working team, each with an equal share in the work and profits eventually, if any. Myself supplying the pictures, R J Tait as publisher, and Barry Keeley recording and layout. Hopefully the books will be in hardback form with a dust jacket.

So, with the teams' good wishes, we look forward to seeing those who are interested at the launch of the book later in the year.

Alfred Woodward, Editor.

ACKNOWLEDGEMENTS

I would like to express my thanks to all who have helped in the production of this work, there are many who have helped, but no longer with us:

The Birmingham Mail
The Stratford Herald
The Evesham Journal
The Banbury Guardian
The Shakespeare Birthplace Trust
The Warwickshire Records Office
The Worcestershire Records Office
Dugdales Antiquities of Warwickshire
Nash's, Worcestershire
Atkins, Gloucestershire
The Gloucestershire Records Office
The typesetter, Mrs Gillian Bryan
My partners who have been the backbone to this effort.
Canon Nicholas Morgan, St George's Church, Brailes.
My brother, Tom, who has helped with the many names, which appear in the book.
Mrs B Stather
J P B Braddell
Mrs Betty Smith
Mr Ken Durham
Mr Martin Cole
And to any I may have unknowingly omitted.

BRAILES HILL

THE MOST PROMINENT FEATURE IN THE PARISH OF BRAILES. It rises to 800 feet above sea level and can be seen for miles in almost every direction, with a very steep SCARP on all sides, the first element in this history may therefore be THE CELTIC BREE; (HILL); Noted under HIGH BRAY (PND57)[1]. Going back if this is correct, the NAME would be very ancient, going back to THE PERIOD when British Names were formed with the Defining Element first; as in the GERMANIC LANGUAGES and not, as in later WELSH; CORNISH; and BRETON. Known today as BRAILES HILL; HILL BARN stands in close proximity to HIGHWALL COPPICE its BEECH TREES standing on a CELTIC BURIAL MOUND; a Celtic Long Barrow.

THE BARN with an enclosed Cattle Yard is all you see today, but at one time, unknown when it was pulled down, stood close to the barn A cottage, a listed building, occupied in 1327 by WILLIAM ATTE HULL.

Welcome to
WARWICKSHIRE
Shakespeare's County

WELCOME TO WARWICKSHIRE marks the BORDER between OXFORDSHIRE and WARWICKSHIRE.
Below is the start of HANGING DITCH LANE, a green road running down to Traitor's Ford, the south-east corner of the Parish of Brailes. Somewhere along this lane it is believed the Brailes Gallows could be found, the last person hung on the gallows was about mid-19th Century for setting fire to a hay rick.

TRAITOR'S FORD crosses the road at the south eastern edge of the Parish of Brailes, named after a previous owner of Aitchill Farm, Mr Traitor. Through the iron gate into a field called HIGHSTREET, follow the hedgerow on the right, and this will take you to HANGING DITCH LANE, follow this lane up to the main Brailes to Banbury road on the boundary line. Follow the course of this ancient trackway, and it takes you past EDGEHILLS TOWER to CAMP LANE, follow this for about half a mile or so and at a steep corner you can see from the roadside ARLESCOTE VILLAGE from what was once an Iron-Age Camp Site.

GALLOWAYS HILLS FARM lies below the road well sheltered from the north and easterly winds. About a field away you could find the spring, which feeds the lake built on COMBSLADE FARM at the north-east corner of Fishers Coppice. This stream was the source of power which drove the MEDIAEVAL WATER MILL. BRAILES MILL, about a field-length away on the south side of the road to Traitor's Ford. The River Stour from its source in the Parish of Sibford, runs just behind the hedgerow in the hollow into which the stream empties after running past the Mill.

Above: ADDENES HILL BARN on GALLOWS HILL FARM. Not far from the barn is a spring, the source of the small stream which runs through the centre of the farmyard at COMBSLADE FARM, down to FISHERS COPPICE where a man-made trout lake can be seen, then under the Brailes to Hook Norton road and runs past the old MEDIAEVAL MILL SITE before entering the River Stour. Supplied water power for the Mill. Below: the map will show you the course of the stream, and also the route of DITCHEDGE LANE, often called Hanging Ditch Lane, crosses the Banbury road at the boundary.

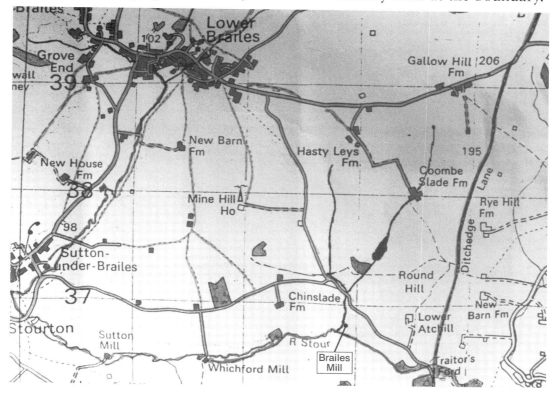

BRICKYARD COTTAGE before its enlargement, situated at the foot of Brickyard Hill close the road entrance to Combslade Farm. This brickyard was part of the Brailes House Estate, owned by H J SHELDON. It was purchased in 1902 by Miss Nelson, who then owned what was left of the original Manor of Brailes, and the end of this once vast estate was sold to individuals at her death in 1920. Mostly by sitting tenants. Below shows what remains of the brickworks owned by Florence Wilkes, no mention of her husband, Thomas, with this works. Mr Thomas Neal purchased this farm inclusive of the brickworks, no longer operational. The brick kilns were pulled down in 1943 by Mr Harold Neal, who had inherited the farm.

HOLLOWAY HILL picture shows MR JOHN BRYAN of Brailes on his way to work on Galloways Hill Farm. At one time 30-to-40 men and boys worked on this farm. The Hill was named after ROBERT de HOLEWEYE 1327-1332, a later report by Mr B G Charles informs us that the HOLEWEYE FAMILY were still living at the foot of Holloway Hill in 1419. MRS THOMAS FIELD, who lived in The Park during the 1920's, remembered remains of Cottages at the foot of the Hill during her lifetime, also remains of houses in the field known as SPOONERS HOUSE GROUND on the south side of the LITTLE PARK, also on the south side of the Banbury Road.

Above: A view of THE LITTLE PARK on the opposite side of the road to its larger relative, THE PARK. You can see where the original track way enters this field at the corner of the houses to the left of the brick-built house owned by Frank Miller, the lone figure of a sheep is the sole occupant.

Below: THE PARK pictured from HOLLOWAY HILL, about the best picture to show the field as it once was, NO HOUSES, and the Salt Road, which runs through to THE SALT WORKS at DROITWICH clearly shown.

A PRETTY VIEW OF BRAILES - 20

Top View showing from off the top of the hill above THE PARK a view of the north and north-east side. The view was taken in the early-1930's.

Bottom View shows the old thatched houses etc., which run alongside what was the Farm Road to Rectory Farmhouse. The Elm Trees are all gone.

Two views of THE PARK, Lower Brailes prior to the 1930's, when the first Council Houses began to appear. At the present time the lower half lying west of the Old Salt Road is now full of Council Houses and bungalows.

The Salt Road can be see running along in front of Houses on the eastern side of the road.

Above is the view travellers get of Lower Brailes when exiting from Holloway Hill, a far different view when looking at it today minus all the Elm trees, which made this part of Brailes so attractive.

The card below gives a nice picture of the OLD SALT ROAD, travelled along by people since the second Century. In 1240 20 pack horse loads of salt would arrive from DROITWICH SALT WORKS, payment to the King for timber he had sold to the works from the large woods he owned at Tanworth-in-Arden

The first Council Houses to be built close to The Park, facing onto the Banbury Road. Two out of four are shown. The first family to move into No 1 was Frank Hibberd with his wife Muriel, nee Sparks. Frank had retired from the Birmingham City Police and moved back to his home town. Daughter, Evelyn, and sons, Douglas, Sydney, and Clemence. In No 2, was Alwyn Claydon and his wife.

RECTORY FARMHOUSE was home for the BISHOP family. William Bishop lived there from 1554-1624, and after the Reformation he became ROMAN CATHOLIC BISHOP OF ALL ENGLAND. He was BISHOP OF CHALCEDON. The Roman Catholic Church was given by the Bishop family for the Catholic Community of Brailes Parish. The interior of the Church was a beautiful place to worship in, as the accompanying pictures will show. As well as giving the Church, beneath it a Malt House, the family gave donations towards the upkeep of BRAYLES GRAMMAR SCHOLE, which dates back to 1533. THE PRIEST'S HOUSE faces onto CARRY HAY, a white-fronted house, just south of the cottage door is a stone flight of steps running up to the Church. FATHER JOHN AUSTIN died on 27th August 1809, aged 68 years. The tablet bearing this inscription is on the EXTERIOR WALL of the CHANCEL at the EAST END of ST GEORGE'S CHURCH, often referred to as THE CATHEDRAL OF THE FELDON. The Feldon being one of the richest tracts of land in the County of Warwickshire, running from close to Sutton-under-Brailes across to Aylesmore Farm. His TABLE TOMB is only a few yards away from the above tablet.

MR AND MRS CHARLES HEWS pictured outside Rectory Farmhouse in the early-20th Century, 1900-1920.

Below is the KITCHEN ENTRANCE to Rectory Farmhouse, running away from it THE MALT HOUSE with the Catholic Church of ST PETER AND ST PAUL above it. The last residents of Rectory Farmhouse were Mr and Mrs Philip Suffolk. Mrs Suffolk repaired almost every book in the Church's possession, an extremely and valuable one.

THE CHURCH'S INTERIOR - Circa 1920's and 1930's

THE HOME for the Catholic Priest of St Peter's and St Paul's Church.
Above: WILLIAM BISHOP DD, born at Rectory Farm, Lower Brailes 1554.
The first Catholic Bishop consecrated for England and Scotland after the
Reformation. Died 13th April 1624, aged 71 years. Buried in the Chancel
before the altar in St George's Church, Brailes.

Left: The entrance to St Peter's and St Paul's Catholic Church, Friars Lane, Lower Brailes.

Manuscript fetches £23,000

The earliest - known work by England's first professional illuminator — William de Brailes from Brailes, near Banbury — has been sold at Sotheby's for £23,000.

The manuscript, written and illuminated in Oxford in the early 13th century, went to a London dealer, Mr Bernard Quaritch, on Monday after brisk bidding.

A Sotheby's spokesman described the price as "a very good one."

William de Brailes was an Oxford layman, who worked in Catte Street and also on the site of All Souls Chapel. The manuscript comprises 440 vellum leaves and is a portable Bible in latin.

It has 38 large painted initials in colour, many incorporating dragons, lions, birds and crouching pheasants. It also has 48 other large initials and one miniature.

Right: A photograph of a newspaper cutting recording of a LOST VILLAGE TREASURE. A PORTABLE BIBLE in LATIN containing 440 vellum leaves, 38 leaves adorned with initials in colour depicting dragons, lions, birds, and crouching pheasants with just one small miniature. This beautiful manuscript Bible was the work of a Brailes man, WILL de BRAYLES, a 13th Century artist born in BRAYLES, but in later life he lived and worked in CATTE STREET, OXFORD on the site of ALL SOULS CHAPEL. An illuminator of Mediaeval Illuminated Manuscripts, few of his works are known. Ones that have survived can be best described as rare works of art. This Bible was sold by FATHER CORNICK as Priest in Charge to SIR THOMAS PHILLIPS of MIDDLE HILL, BROADWAY for the sum of £200 in the 1930's, and placed along with other treasures he had purchased in THIRLESTAINE HOUSE, CHELTENHAM. After Sir Thomas Phillips' death in 1872 this collection was sold by THE LONDON BOOKHOUSE William H Robinson for £23,000. The whole collection was sold in stages over the following years.

The Foundation that was responsible for the Grammar Schole dates back to 1533 in the reign of King Henry VIII. A grant was given in 1537 by the Master and Wardens of THE GUILD OF ST MARY, founded and maintained in St George's Church, Lower Brailes of £8 1s 8d to JOHN PITTES, Clerk and School Master. This was the Boys' School until circa 1903 and in that year boys and girls were amalgamated, the girls and infants school in Sheep Street, and the boys in what is known as The Boys School at the eastern edge of the Churchyard. THE GRAMMAR SCOLE was listed as a school with House and Garden for the Master, a record of the later school dates back to mid-to-second half of the 19th Century. Pictured above Master and Boys circa 1903.

Above: The first garage in Brailes owned and run by Mr Cecil Righton.

Below: Some views of the site where RODNEY WILKES had a butcher's shop. This was at the turn of the century, circa 1903, for Rodney owned a motor car in that year. I do not know the exact year the business closed down, but I was told that Rodney committed suicide. This was told to me by an old resident of Brailes, long since passed away.   Two more buildings on the site, and many old remains of motor cars, put there initially by Cecil when in an unroadworthy condition.

More buildings on the site of Rodney Wilks's butcher's shop, which was in existence over 100 years ago. It looks as if they are at the rear of what was the actual shop.

RODNEY WILKS was the owner of a 1903 Daimler car, but neither of the two scrap cars are Daimlers, just two which Cecil Righton had scrapped after removing parts from them to fit on other vehicles.

Top picture was the home of Mr Joe Warmington and family. The kitchen had been built over a well, which was underneath the kitchen table. In the corner was a copper and with a red tiled floor it was wash day in comfort, water in abundance with just a few feet to carry it.

Below: Where COW LANE ends and the main Banbury road to cross then along the century's old SALT ROAD. Cow Lane 1410 to 1696. This old road was the main road through Lower Brailes, then the road ran past The George Hotel. The present-day road was made from Banbury to Shipston-on-Stour in the early-19th Century.

LOWER BRAILES

Minehill Home Farmhouse, the scene of a sad event on 24th October 1941, for into the garage on the left of the farmhouse were taken the bodies of five airmen, who had died in a fatal air crash taken by the burnt out remains of Wellington Bomber Mk 1c "B" flight, take off was from the aerodrome in Shennington, with six crew members and one airman hitching a lift to advance his training, frequently done at many training stations. The actual crew were Sgt S King, Screen Pilot fully trained, Sgt Thackwell, trainee pilot in charge of the aircraft, Sgt's C H Webb and C K Butt, observers/wireless operators, also doubling as bomb aimers, Sgt R W Campbell severely injured, died of his injuries on the morning of 25th October 1941. Rear Gunner Sgt S T Baverstock also badly injured, the sole survivor, who told us it took ten months before he fully recovered. He then returned to his duties and served the remainder of the war in India. The unknown airman who had hitch-hiked, also died in the crash. In 1999, Sgt S T Baverstock retired, returned to Brailes in 1999, and visited the woman who had nursed him on the fateful night of 24th October and told his listeners the true story of how the aircraft crashed, confirming that seven airmen were on board the plane that night.

Above: PLUM TREE, The home of Mr Chris Righton in Cow Lane. Originally three cottages, with some of the original features which date back to the 14th Century, house or houses on site the age of the Church.

Below: A 1905 view of the Church taken from Cow Lane. View was taken from Sheep Street, side of Plum Tree. Tenants at the time were The Hancocks and Parkers. Mr Leonard Truby farmed Mill Hill Home Farm.

Above: WORKHOUSE ROW after the disastrous fire in the early-1950's. Sunday morning, bells ringing for Church, but that morning most of the villagers were helping the tenants get their household goods from the houses.

Below: The houses built on the site, photo taken from the front of Plum Tree House. The drive which ran along the rear of Workhouse Row was a private drive to Minehill Home Farmhouse and not, as people might have thought, a public right of way.

THE WILLOWS where for many years Mr Thomas Morley lived. I worked for him after school and at weekends for 2s 6d. I was sacked after he caught me knocking an apple off one of the trees. I found out that Bill Phillips and my elder brother, Tom, were also sacked and for the same reason. He never paid us the 2s 6d we had earned during the week - always a weekend sacking!

The Old Cottage was finally taken down. I believe the old fireplace and wooden beams were retained in that end of the new house, not finished shown below, the house on the opposite page.

A workshop was also built at the southern end of the new house. I was supposed to have gone along and taken pictures of the finished buildings.

I will take you back to the second century, to a time when the Old Salt Road was used by everyone who wished to leave the Town of Brailes. A large ROMAN CAMP existing at DAWN on the outskirts of Moreton-in-Marsh. The Romans would have used the track way, for from the FOSSEWAY they could cross the RIVER STOUR via the FORD at WILLINGTON, or FAMINGTON FARM a short stretch of a MINOR ROMAN ROAD is shown on the map. The track way then continued over Brailes Hill to the Town of Brailes. LOWER BRAILES ended over 100 yards beyond the BRIDGE, OVER BRAYLES or Upper Brailes began just beyond the entrance into what was the Timber Yard for the BRAILES HOUSE ESTATE. ATTWOODS HOUSE on the corner of Sutton Lane was not built until the mid-19th Century. Hedges on either side of the road from where Over Brayles began. COW LANE was mentioned as the main route through Lower Brayles after the travellers had followed Sheep Street and the track way down to the beginning of Cow Lane after crossing the small stream running through WHEATLEY CLOSE named THE LAPSTONE. If you follow the track way after passing Almedow Farm and arriving at Epwell Whitehouse, you will find the Romans built a section of road, and also had a village, and fortifications on MAD MARSTON HILL so you can see the importance of these early track ways. Cow Lane as you see it today.

2

It is difficult to see when looking at the picture on your left, that this pathway was during the 1930's. It was wide enough for a horse and cart to travel along it with ease, entry to what is known as WHEATLEY CLOSE was through a gateway with a five-bar gate stopping cattle from getting out of the field. Grass mown and turned into hay. The section running down to Cow Lane was a lot wider, a tarred and gravel path some three-to-four feet wide, and the grass verge was mown and wide enough for us to play cricket on. Channels cut by the road men to drain the water off the path, running into a ditch alongside it.

SHIPESTRETE = SHEPESTRETE
SHEEP STREET = SCHOOL LANE.

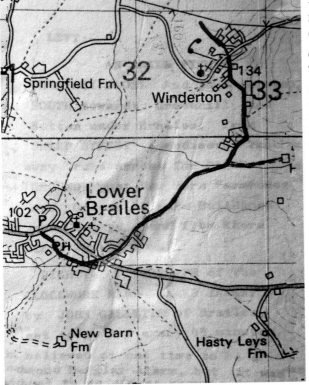

Referred to as the Main Road running via this Street down to COW LANE, follow this to its eastern end, passing the way to THE WILLOWS, PLUM TREE COTTAGES, MINE HILL HOME FARMHOUSE and the many new houses built in recent years, JOE WARMINGTON'S HOUSE, and the NEW HOUSES in an adjoining paddock, then crossing today's Main Road to follow the OLD SALT ROAD to WINDERTON, or take the Farm Road to ALLMEADOW FARM and then to EPWELL WHITE HOUSE and on to BANBURY, where you travel into Banbury from the top of Constitution Hill. This track way would take you to THE WASH in Norfolk.

3

Above: A view of THE GREEN, Lower Brailes when the large Elm trees were still standing, their lives cut short by Dutch Elm Disease.

Below: THE WHEELWRIGHT'S SHOP in 1850. Mr J Davis was at work in this shop, and in 1874 was joined by his two sons, RICHARD AND THOMAS. They continued to trade until 1902, when Ernest Godson was listed as Wheelwright at Lower Brailes. In 1923 the business was closed, Ernest had sold out to his relative at Upper Brailes. Nothing could be seen of the lovely old house behind the workshops until they were pulled down.

The Green, Lower Brailes.

Summer and winter views of this lost trade, for very few horses are used by farmers and business people today. By the mid-1930's the roadside buildings had been pulled down, just the thatched roof WAGGON SHED remains to remind us of the lost business. With the buildings pulled down a wall was built, where they once stood the section of railings were left. The following pictures will reveal what had been hidden from sight.

The Morland Series

Lower Brailes.

This lovely thatched house was once hidden from view from off the Main Street, hidden from view behind the Old Wheelwright's Shop until the 1920's, fondly remembered as FATHER BROWN'S home, a Catholic Priest. In his and in later years until it was made unlawful, THE WAGGON SHED in which new and old ones repaired would be new and old farm wagons and carts. On Corpus Christi Sunday a portable altar would be erected and, when the Corpus Christi Procession arrived at this point, a short service would be held.

After the service the procession would continue its journey across WEST ORCHARD to the Church of St Peter and St Paul. Above shows Father Brown's Cottage after a fall of snow. The Stores just below, also snowed up, owners over the years were James West 1910/20, Mrs Cuthbert 1930's, Miss Hitchman, Phyllis Harris, and Ian Haycock. Behind the Store were several houses in what is called THE BULLRING.

The Corpus Christi Procession coming down Stockstury Hill, flower petals strewn almost the full route the procession had taken, strewn on the road. A group of villagers at the foot of Friars Lane, bypassed on this occasion. Boys walking along the path were Thomas Boyce, Henry Warmington, and Marshall Green - in front Alfred Woodward and Walter Cummings.

Two scarce views of the rear of Father Brown's Cottage with a typical country-style garden. Bottom view shows that the thatched roof has been renewed.

A typical picture in the 1930's and 1940's seeing Harold Mathews's buses parked almost side-by-side outside his home, preparing to set out for their Banbury runs. Carts and tractors close to the Cummings's Forge, and a car parked while its owner did some shopping at Miss Hitchman's stores. Below the store when it was owned by Mr and Mrs Smith.

A reminder to those who do not know about the Sunday morning in the 1950's when WORKHOUSE ROW was burnt down leaving the stone walls standing. The bottom picture shows the firemen from Shipston-on-Stour still damping down the smouldering ruins, only two of the cottages were rebuilt, converted into one larger house to which the owner, Mrs Leonard Truby, returned to, to live in her new home. The private drive to MINEHILL HOME FARM was closed.

Top picture shows in the left foreground the home of Henry Godson, who once inherited the CARRIER BUSINESS at Lower Brailes. He sold the business to Richard Mathews in the early 20th Century. Mathews Coach can be seen standing outside the home where the Mathews's lived. Bottom shows Adkins and Thomas's steam wagon opposite the Godson's home. Arrow indicates which house.

This OLD SMITHY has been in almost daily use for the last 350 years. A part of the old TOWN OF BRAYLES, for the Old Trackway ran along the front of a row of three cottages into SPOONERS HOUSE GROUND in which as late as the 1930's/'940's a shell of houses could be seen some three feet in height. Over the following years this old building stone has been carted away for repair work or for the construction of new houses and are no longer visible above ground as in previous years. In 1868, when much of the Old Town existed, JOHN MORLEY was owner of this SMITHY. He handed the business down to his son, Thomas MORLEY, who in 1911 sold the Smithy and goodwill to ALFRED CUMMINGS, and the business has remained in the ownership of this family until the present day. Douglas, when he took over the family business, went modern and began to do repair work to tractors and more work on farm machinery. Finally, Douglas opened up a garage close to Friars Lane, and this is still active today, known as THE FORGE GARAGE.

The Home where the CUMMINGS FAMILY lived. ALFRED CUMMINGS purchased the SMITHY and goodwill of the business run by John and Thomas Morley since 1868 until son, Thomas, sold to Alfred Cummings. To the right of the van, you first had the SMITHY adjoining the house and outbuildings and then right of the entrance to the yard, MISS JANET MORLEY'S home. She had worked as a nurse in London at a well-known children's hospital, then during the 1939/45/46 war, knew what it was like going into the underground stations to escape the bombing from German aircraft.

42

Top: From the left THE OLD POST OFFICE, Post Master Clark Pickering. SADDLERS THATCH where WILLIAM ARNETT was saddler in 1874, then circa 1888 J T JARVIS became Brailes and District SADDLER and lived at Brailes until his death in the 1950's. He was aged 85 years when he died in 1953.

Bottom: From Saddlers Thatch the first House past the blue door was where Doctor Thomas Henry Hitchins lived when he first arrived in Brailes, to take over Doctor Cawley's practice, having retired in that year, 1850, and he died in 1898.

A BRAILES MYSTERY BUILDING. No-one appears to know what its original use was. STONE COPING and WINDOWSILLS, slated roof, and bricked-in windows, no reason why this was done for Window Tax no longer existed. I know for certain that at times when The George Inn, later to become a hotel, outbuildings were filled to overflowing with WOOL, during the lucrative years, when wool growing as rearing sheep for their wool, was known. Wool was stored until collected after being brought in by the Parish Farm Community was one use it had. I believe this particular building has all the hallmarks of having been built for the receiving and delivery of MAIL, during the 19th Century in particular when coaches were carrying almost all the mail, as they travelled the length and breadth of the country.

During the war years and for some years after, Mrs Cecil Righton was garaging her motor car in the building, renting it from Clark Pickering, who owned and ran the Post Office on the opposite side of the road. So perhaps the idea that it was a Mail House may be correct.

THIS OLD COTTAGE with a timber outbuilding on which countless numbers of notices were posted, until forbidden by Charles and Eva Mumford, a preservation order would have been a better proposition than permission to pull it down to build a modern bungalow on the site. This type of cottage was the usual type of house where working-class people were housed, and still the houses of this type are being destroyed by builders who have no conscience - part of the age when BRAYLES was a TOWN second only to Warwick in importance, Birmingham still a small village, the TOWN CRIER'S BELL in St George's Church still reminds us of those days. The STOCKS once attached to an Elm tree on The Green close to the Church went when the tree was felled in the 19th Century. The Reverend Nicholas Morgan when he appeared on a SCHOOLS RECORDING OF BRAILES showing details of the DOMESDAY PERIOD when William the Conqueror became the man to record the whole country, showing it in what became known as THE HUNDRED ROLLS, and people are still trying to record the past, for the future at present looks rather bleak for all concerned.

Upon reflection I must admit that the Bungalow which replaced the old cottage would be the choice of most people, unless one happened to be a person who wanted something entirely different.

Below shows a group of children playing in the field at the rear of the old cottage. The only one I know is Phyllis Harris, back row third from the left. In winter the ground behind them would be full of water, despite the ditch which runs from it into THE LAPSTONE running through Wheatley Close.

PAST AND PRESENT. Top picture shows the Old Post Office at Lower Brailes, when Clark Pickering was Post Master and like his father, Thomas, who he succeeded, were both Church Wardens at St George's Church, Brailes. In the centre of the road on this picture is Joe Dawson's bakery van. It looks as if they were having starting trouble! Below how the Old Post Office has been modernised - porch, front door, and windows all changed. I have a small book entitled ALONE IN LONDON, presented to William Pickering Brailes, Church Sunday School Award 1870.

On the opposite side of the road from this old Thatched House was a row of thatched cottages showing that this was part of the Old Town of Brailes. Many of the older parts of the town vanished for ever after the new road was built from Banbury to Shipston-on-Stour, begun at Banbury about 1840, date of completion unknown. The village green on which the Cenotaph was erected in 1922 was where the ANNUAL HORSE FAIR was held as early as the 16th Century. A horse thief was arrested at this fair while trying to sell a stolen horse, and tried and gaoled at Warwick Assizes.

THE FORGE GARAGE now occupies the site of the old houses, and perhaps that may explain why Mr Joseph Dawson's property was once a PUBLIC HOUSE named THE POLEAXE. For with an annual fair and the Sheep Market most likely held in what is known as Wheatley Close, THE GEORGE INN and THE ROSE and CROWN INN are close to both the Market Sites, together with THE POLEAXE pictured below.

The SMALL TOWN GREEN at the side of the main road by STOCKSTURY
HILL, with Elm Trees on it and attached to the foot of one THE BRAYLES
STOCKS, as early as the 16th Century a scene of great activity once a year
when the ANNUAL HORSE FAIR was held on it, THE GEORGE HOTEL
and an old ale house named THE POLEAXE stood at either end of the Green
so plenty of refreshments for buyers and sellers. The Stocks disappeared
when the Elm tree was felled in the mid-1800's, about the same time as the
history of the Stone I am about to write about. Close to the side entrance of
the village Institute, which stands at the eastern end of the green you will find
a stone, standing behind some iron railings. The inscription on it reads:

BANBURY
To
SHIPSTON
Brailes

It was formerly a stone step at the front of THE ROSE AND CROWN INN,
then named PARK VIEW and finally Blenhiem House, home of SANDY
DELLER. The iron railings, gate, and gate posts were erected for THOMAS
UPTON, owner of the Inn in the 19th Century. The builder had used the stone
showing no inscriptions on it to rest the gate posts of wrought or cast iron on.
These items were pulled down sometime in 1939/45 as a WAR EFFORT, the
iron to be used for making War Material, which I later found out was of no
use, so all the wrought iron taken down in those years was after the war
loaded onto ships and dumped out at sea. In 1999 Sandy decided to erect
some iron railings with gate and posts as the original had been. The stone step
was removed, and it was then that Sandy saw the inscriptions, the RECORDS
OFFICE at Warwick supplied the following information:
BANBURY TO BARCHESTON (Shipston) TURN PIKE TOLL ROAD
TRUST that a MEETING was held at THE GEORGE HOTEL in 1802.
JAMES UPTON, landlord, was to set a toll, which he priced at £86.00. The
lettering minus any mileage was obviously a Mile Stone, originally placed
unknown. Further research required to know exactly where if possible.

LOWER BRAILES

Above THE ROSE AND CROWN
INN, Landlord Owner, Thomas
Upton showing the stone under
discussion as it was found a STONE
STEP, placed there at the time the
railings and gate were erected in the
1800's. Removed during the War
Years 1939/40's and new railings
and gate erected in the 1990's when
the stone on the left was discovered
to be a MILESTONE several
centuries old. Back at least, I
imagine, to the Coaching Era......

BRAILES INSTITUTE V A HOSPITAL (CLASS A) was changed from a place of entertainment into a hospital of ten beds.

V A D WARWICK 48

Commander Miss Dickins

Quarter Master Mrs Findlay

Medical Officer George Findlay M A, M B C S

Training Nurse Sister Owen

V A D Nursing Staff

Mrs F Gander, Mrs S Garrard, Miss K Gibbs, Mrs L M Potter, Mrs E Spencer, Miss E Stevens, Mrs M Sutton, Miss J Sutton, (Cook) Miss C Lees

Helpers.

During the time the hospital has been opened the Nursing Staff also included Mrs E Burnham, Miss R Dickins, Miss A Mathews, Mrs A Wheeler.

And Cooks

Lady Harvey, Miss E Smith, Miss S Smith.

V A D Warwick/15

Section Leader E R Gander.

Orderlies: A H Cummings, G Field, T Ivens, J Crook, Rev F E Garrard, F T Jarvis, W Clay, H Gregory, T Morby, E Clay, A J Gould, E Pickering, T Cullen, E Hemming, J Webb.

THE INSTITUTE V A HOSPITAL, BRAILES

Date of Opening - 28th October 1914

Attached to the Southern General Hospital. Accommodation - ten beds. The Institute V A D originally opened for convalescent Belgian soldiers. Since June 1915 it has received British patients throughout Birmingham.

Total Admissions	-	83
Discharges fit for duty	-	71
To Medical Boards	-	3
Transfers	-	3
Deaths	-	Nil
In Hospital 31st March 1916	-	6
Total	-	83

THE INSTITUTE V A HOSPITAL, BRAILES (CLASS A).
Below (left) Dr George Findlay M A, M B, C M, Medical Officer.
Below (right) Mrs Harriet Findlay, quarter master.

Section Leader E R Gander, Orderlies: A H Cummings, G Field, T Ivens, J Crook, Rev F E Garrard, F T Jarvis, W Clay, H T Morby, E Clay, A J Gould, E Pickering, T Cullen, E Hemming, J Webb. Bottom: The Nurses.

Above: Rev F E Garrard, Orderly: Mrs Stella Garrard, Nurse.
Below left: Miss Dorothy Garrard, Nurse at the V A D Hospital Institute, Brailes.

Top picture: The first intake of wounded Belgian soldiers at the INSTITUTE V A HOSPITAL. The first one in the County of Warwickshire. Supported by people of Ascott, Whichford, Cherington, Stourton, Sutton-under-Brailes, and Brailes with Winderton. Farmers donated eggs and other produce to the hospital.

Bottom picture: Shows another group of wounded soldiers taken with the nurses who were caring for them.

THE STRAKER STEAM OMNIBUS which arrived in Shipston-on-Stour 3rd September 1903. Made a trial run to Lower Brailes on 11th September 1903. Started its service run from Lower Brailes to Stratford Station on 16th September 1903. Charge 1d per mile. From Lower Brailes the cost was 4d. I have the first 4d ticked purchased by Mr Fred Gander to ensure he had a seat for this first run.

THE STRAKER STEAM OMNIBUS pictured outside the rear entrance to
THE GEORGE HOTEL, Church Street, Shipston-on-Stour circa 1903/05.

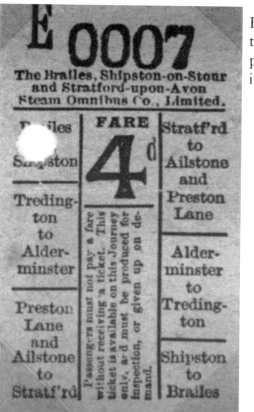

Bottom: Copy of the TIMETABLE on
the right. Ticket a copy of the 4d ticket
purchased by Fred Gander of Brailes for
its first maiden run.

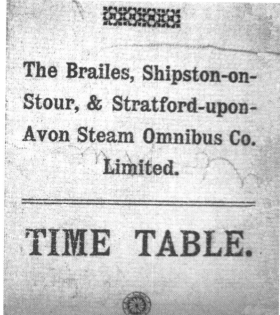

FROM	Every Day. a.m.	Every Day except Friday. p.m.	Fridays only. p.m.	FROM	Every Day. a.m.	Every Day except Thurs. p.m.	Thursday only. p.m.
Brailes (George Inn) ...	7 40	2 40*		Stratford (G.W.R. Stat'n)	10 50	5 15	6 15
Shipston-on-Stour ...	8 15	3 15	1 0	Stratford (Plym'th Arms)	11 0	5 30	6 20
Honington Turnpike ...	8 20	3 20	1 5	Ailstone ...	11 15	5 45	6 35
Tredington (White Lion)	8 30	3 30	1 15	Preston Lane ...	11 20	5 50	6 40
Half'rd & Armsc'tt Turn	8 35	3 35	1 20	Wimpstone Lane ...	11 25	5 52	6 45
Newbold (Bird-in-Hand)	8 45	3 45	1 30	Alderminster (Bell) ...	11 35	6 5	6 50
Alderminster (Bell) ...	9 0	4 0	1 45	Newbold (Bird-in-Hand)	11 50	6 20	7 5
Wimpstone Lane ...	9 5	4 5	1 50	Half'rd & Armsc'tt Turn	11 55	6 25	7 10
Preston Lane ...	9 10	4 10	1 55	Tredington (White Lion)	12 5 p.m.	6 35	7 2
Ailstone ...	9 15	4 15	2 0	Honington Turnpike ...	12 10	6 40	7 2
Stratford (Plym'th Arms)	9 30	4 30	2 20	Shipston-on-Stour ..	12 15	6 50	7 3
Stratford (G.W.R. Stat'n)	9 35	4 35	2 25	Brailes (George Inn) ...	1 0*	7 20	8 5

* Wednesdays and Saturdays only.

Return Tickets can be taken and Seats booked for Return Journey at the ordinary fare.
Parcels will be carried at ordinary rates, and may be left at the stopping-places for collection, and arrangements will be made for delivery.

For further Information apply to the Conductor, or
O. T. BURNHAM, Manager.
G. S. MARTIN, Secretary.

Offices: Church Street, Shipston-on-Stour,

Top: Copy of the original timetable in my possession. O T Burnham Manager. G S Smith Secretary. Steam Omnibus Service between Brailes and Stratford-upon-Avon.

SHIPSTON TRAM by OLD SUMMERTON

Whatever will poor Shipston do
Shareholders and the Country too
The Omnibus has gone.

The traffic on the road don't pay
She's now cut off, right straightaway
She's doomed to no more runs
Tis not the many, but the few
To whom the enterprise is due
All known to such men
The scheme has failed like schemes before

And thus the failure we deplore
Let's hope they'll try again
The lost convenience we regret
For certainly it somewhat met
A transit years delayed
Communication day by day
With the larger towns away
To stimulate the trade
A little rhyme I learnt at school
Be this the company's golden rule
And try, try, try again
They know poor Shipston stands in need.
Then let them try till they succeed
With all their might and main

Written by the Late L T Summerton senior on the discontinuance of the Steam Bus Service between Shipston, Brailes, and Stratford. Published in the Evesham Standard 16th September 1905. A service which began October 1903. Service ended 16th September 1905.

STEPHEN STEEL, Willington and Shipston-on Stour CARRIER CART late
HENRY GODSON'S of Lower Brailes. George Field of Brailes, roundsman
for this carrier business, married Stephen's daughter, Miss Amy Steel, circa
1900. The first I know of Mr George Field is that he was a married man
living with his wife in Workhouse Row and was working for Mr Leonard
Truby on Mine Hill Home Farm at Lower Brailes 1920's/30's. He moved in
later life to Fenny Compton, but members of his family are still living in
Brailes and Shipston-on-Stour.

A R SPICER, CARRIER Upper Brailes. The picture shown above was when A R Spicer was in Banbury. He did most of his carrier business in Shipston-on-Stour, picking up what the residents of Brailes had ordered from the travelling salesmen from several of the family businesses.

Below: RICHARD MATHEWS with the Horse Drawn carrier cart he had purchased from Henry Godson. Richard later sold this carrier cart to Stephen Steel of Willington.

BRAYLES

Scarce & aged in black & white - Revised by Braywood

Page 4 - Coombe Slade Farm

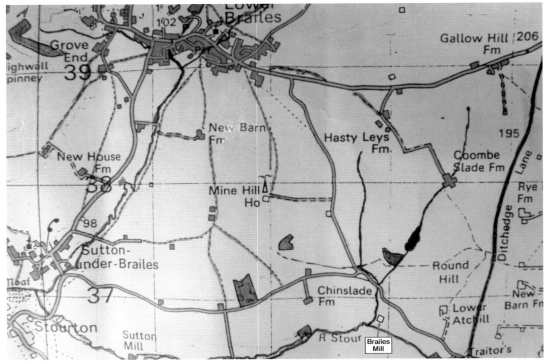

Page 5 - Brayles Medieval Mill

Page 33 - Browns Cottage

Page 33

The Green, Lower Brailes.

Page 1 - Highwall Spinney

Page 177 - Crooks Slauter House

Page 28 - Cow Lane

Page 29

Page 36

Page 37 - Smiths Shop

High Street, Brailes

After Harold Mathews returned from the 1914/18 War he joined his father in the carrier business. In 1923 Harold decided to become more modern in his method of business and so he purchased a 14-seater model T Ford in 1923 and, as we already know, the horse-drawn carts were sold.

A Utility model he purchased just after the 1939/45 War. This had wooden, slatted seats, uncomfortable to sit on, but in the 1960's he had invested in a modern Bedford Coach as seen in the bottom picture.

MRS HARRIET MUMFORD seated by the side of her daughter-in-law, MRS EVA MUMFORD, wife of CHARLES MUMFORD. In front of the old thatched cottage, which stood opposite the Forge Garage in Lower Brailes. Later pulled down as explained earlier. Harriet Mumford for many years was looked upon as the village midwife. In later years, with failing eyesight, she could no longer do the work she had loved to do. HARRIET MUMFORD was one of the Brailes Centenarians. Harriet died on 17th May 1945, aged 100 years, having lived through two wars. I would have loved to have met and recorded the changes she had seen at Brailes during her lifetime and how many births she had been present at. Eva and Charles Mumford had no children of their own, but adopted a step-daughter. What they would have thought about the pulling down of this small cottage they had called home will never be known.

Right: The family tombstone to be found on the right side of the path running through the churchyard, which is also the way to the 109 steps, today 122.

TO THE GLORIOUS MEMORY OF THOSE WHO LAID DOWN THEIR LIVES FOR THEIR COUNTRY IN THE GREAT WAR 1914-1919 FROM THE PARISH OF BRAILES AND WINDERTON.

WALTER ELLIOT, WILLIAM REASON, JOSEPH ALEXANDER, ERNEST AUSTIN, WALTER BOX, OWEN BRADLEY, JONATHAN WING CLAYTON, WILLIAM HENRY CLIFTON, BERT FAIRBROTHER, WILLIAM FIELD, CHARLES HEMMINGS, THOMAS JEFFS, FRANCES JOSEPHN SPENCER, ARTHUR CHARLES SPICER, HENRY WALKER.

Greater love hath no man than this, that a man lay down his life for his friends.

1939 - 1945

JOSEPH HARRIS, FRANCIS FOWLER, CECIL HIBBERD.
They also made The Supreme Sacrifice, laying down their lives that we might live.

CHURCH & VICARAGE. BRAILES.

Above: The Old BRAILES RECTORY. Now converted into flats with St George's Church in the background, and today's RECTORY, entrance to it is off Friars Lane. I was asked the origin of this name. They were Feoffe House, six in number. Years ago some of the old cottages had the Friars living in them. They assisted the Priest-in-Charge. Some of them preaching in Chantry Chapels at Upper Chelmscote and Winderton. Sites are known as Chelmscote, unknown at Winderton. Today's resident priest is CANON NICHOLAS MORGAN.

Rev Thomas Smith 1856-1886. Mary Ann Smith, wife.

Below: Rev F E Garrard with his wife, nee Miss Harriet Woolley Smith, fifth daughter of Thomas and Mary above. Taken on their wedding day, 15th August 1883.

BRAILES. THE WAR MEMORIAL AND CHURCH

BRAILES - THE CHURCH AND WAR MEMORIAL

To the Glory and Praise of God, the Parish Church of ST GEORGE was erected in AD 1350 and was fully restored in AD 1879 at a total cost of £5,693 which included special gifts supplied by donors. A total of 18,556 names are on the donors list of which I have an original copy. The Church was re-opened for Divine Service by the Right Reverend Father in God, Henry, Lord Bishop of Worcester on 20th June 1879. Churchwardens: Henry J Sheldon JP, John Spencer. Architect: William Bassett Smith. Builders: Henry Attwood and Son.

Bottom: A snow-clad scene of the War Memorial and vicarage taken by Mr Harry Hemstock 1940's. St George's Church is often referred to as The Cathedral of the Feldon. The Feldon a rich tract of land running from close to Sutton-under-Brailes through to the north-easterly border of the Parish of Brailes, South Warwickshire.

THE NORTH side of St George's Church with a scattering of snow still
showing on the church tower. The large TOMB shown on the bottom picture
is the tomb of Henry James Sheldon. Tomb erected to his memory by his
sister, Isobel. He was last in line and had no children so the Sheldon name no
longer existed after his death in 1902. He was the last LORD OF THE
MANOR of Brailes, which from the time of William Willington, 16th Century,
to William Sheldon, who had married Willington's daughter, until the death
of James, 400 years of Brailes history has revolved around those two families.

Above: The tombstone of HENRY ATTWOOD, builder of Brailes. The only Attwood to be buried in Brailes. The family vault in which the remainder of the Attwood family are buried is on the south side of WINDERTON CHURCH, a church which the Attwood firm and their workforce built. The church was completed in 1879 and is now one of England's redundant ones. The family certainly left their mark in the Annals of Brailes past history.

Above: The TABLE TOMB of Edward Ralph Charles Sheldon, who was known as Edward Sheldon of Brailes House, and his wife, Marcella. Also in the vault was buried one of his sons. Edward and Marcella had eight children, three sons and five daughters. Only three attained the age of 21 years, namely Henry James Sheldon, Edward Ralph Charles, and Isabel. Edward's wife, Marcella, was the daughter of Thomas Meredith Winstanley of Lissen Hall, Co Dublin. Edward was a Church Warden at St George's Church and a Major of the Warwickshire Militia, Deputy Lieutenant of Warwick, Justice of the Peace, and became Member of Parliament for South Warwickshire in 1835. It lasted about 12 months for he died 11th June 1836 aged 54 years. His tomb is shown above. His wife, MARCELLA, changed her faith and became a Catholic. She died at Boulogne, where she had gone to live. H J Sheldon married Alice Mary, widow of William Oakley of Oakley Park, Salop. Henry James Sheldon was bankrupt and the Brailes House Estate was run by solicitors until his death in 1902. Miss Nelson purchased what remained of this estate in 1902, and at her death in 1920 the estate was finally broken up. Most of the sitting tenants purchased the land or property they rented at most likely rock-bottom prices for a lot of the farm buildings etc. had fallen into bad condition and needed money to repair. Some were never repaired, they just collapsed and the stone used for repairing other property.

Left: A picture of the east window in St George's Church, Brailes.

Below: A view of the interior of the Church taken from the front of the altar and showing the west window with its intricate tracery of a perpendicular pattern containing the painted glass fitted by Messrs Ward & Hughes of London at a cost of £170.00. Depicted in its central lights is The Good Shepherd. In the two southern lights Paul Preaching in Athens and Dorcas giving clothes to the poor. In other lights Timothy being instructed in the Scriptures by his mother and grandmother, and Phillip teaching the ETHIOPIAN EUNOCH. The window dedicated in loving memory of Harriet Wincott, who died in 1870. Dedicated to her memory.

TOP: A view of the Chancel taken from the central aisle of St George's Church, showing the old paraffin lamps, which supplied the lighting during the winter months, since replaced with electricity.

Below left: Is a picture of MR FRED HALL standing by the model he had constructed from matchsticks. A Brailes man, who later moved to Shipston-on-Stour. Fred was standing outside the Fried Fish and Chip Shop in Market place and during our conversation he told me that he hardly had any education, suffering from asthma, he told me he could not read or write, but he added "The Good Lord gave me the patience and skill to do this kind of work". He did not know how many hours he had spent doing this one model, but he gave the model to Brailes, and today it stands proudly inside the Church Fred once attended.

THE LITCH GATE outside St George's Church at Lower Brailes was designed by DARCY BRADDELL. The above is a copy of the sketch by the Architect. It was not done on site, but in London. The reason was because the Architect's Uncle was becoming impatient at the delay and so this sketch was done to cool him off. This was the reply:

ARTIST'S IMPRESSION of the LITCH GATE by DARCY BRADDELL. The job was commissioned by his uncle, R W Braddell, whose wife was the daughter of the INCUMBANT who had just died. It was erected to the memory of The Rev Thomas Smith, vicar of Brailes 1856-1886.

The Litch Gate was built in 1910 and dedicated by the Rev Henry Phillpott, Bishop of Worcester.

Designed by Darcy Braddell, Architect.

Built and erected by Henry and Frank Attwood and their workforce.

Timber, tiles, the making and erecting of this Litch Gate, side gates etc was £220.00.

Information provided by Mr J P D Braddell, son of the architect, who has loaned me the original sketch to take copies of to illustrate the work.

Above: The Litch Gate written about on previous page.

Below: The arrival of the BISHOP OF WORCESTER to dedicate the building. Rev F E Garrard and choir can be seen waiting in the churchyard, and members of the public lining the route on the footpath.

Top: The Bishop entering The Litch Gate, a member of the Church Council closes the gates behind him.

Bottom: The Service of Dedication being held inside the churchyard, members of the public lining the path outside and inside the churchyard. A record of another piece of Brailes history.

Two pictures of the Dedication of the British Legion Standard in 1921/22, but it was 20th February 1926 before the BRAILES BRANCH was founded at a meeting held at THE GATE INN, Upper Brailes. There were eight other villages in the South Warwickshire area, who were enrolled in this branch of the British Legion.

INVENTORY TAKEN ON THE DEATH OF THOMAS WYLKES OF THE GEORGE, BRAILES, 1558

REFERENCE DOCUMENT 296B: At The District Probate Registry, Birmingham.

THOMAS WILKES, late deceased in the Parish of Brailes. Appraised by four indifferent men of the Parish, THOMAS BYSCOOP, WYLIAM BARNARD, WYLIAM HYBATE, THOMAS OCLEYE.

In Prinis 3 Hogs, 3 Stones	13/4
In Poultry	3/4
In Corn, six strikes	6/-
<u>In the Parlour</u>	
2 table boards, 4 forms, a folding table, 2 pairs of tressles, a chair, 3 cushions	10/6
<u>In the Bed Chamber</u>	
2 coverlets	price £4 6s 6d
2 feather beds	26/8
4 mattresses	5/-
5 pillows	6/8
2 bolsters	3/-
A tester	1/4
A pair of blankets	2/-
A standing bedstead and a truckle bed	8/-
2 table boards, 4 forms, a chair, a carpet and a little carpet	3/8
<u>In the Next Chamber</u>	
2 feather beds	20/-
A flock bed and a mattress	10/-
3 bolsters	4/-
A pillow	6d
3 coverlets	16/-
3 bedsteads	5/-
A coffer	1/4
<u>In the Next Chamber</u>	
An old feather bed and a mattress	6/8
A coverlet	5/-
A pair of blankets	?
A bolster and 3 pillows	3/-
Item a bedstead	1/-
5 coffers	6/8
<u>In the Little Parlour</u>	
First a chest	4/-
A table and 3 forms	1/4

In the Servants Chamber

A window cloth, a coverlet, a pillow, 2 coffers,
Another old cloth   8/8

In the Chamber Over the Hall

An old flock bed, 2 mattresses, a window cloth,
A tester, 3 bolsters, 3 bedsteads, a coverlet,
2 bedsteads, 2 coffers   23/4

Also in Another Chamber

2 bedsteads   1/4
2 coffers   2/8

In Pewter

First: 16 plates and 2 saucers   26/8
Item: 10 potingers   6/8
Item: 7 potage dishes   3/6
Item: 2 quart pots, 3 pint pots, a penny pot, 2 old
       Quart pots, 7 plates, and a basin   9/-
       6 pewter dishes   4/-
Item: 3 potage dishes   1/-
Item: 3 salt cellars   6d

In Brass

In brass pots 11, a Chasine and a Possinet, a Pye   56/8
8 brass pans   40/-
Item: Challistemes   6/-
Item: 2 skimmers, 2 gosse pans, 2 pairs of cobbes,
       4 brasses, 3 pairs of pot hooks, a fire shovel, a
       pair of tongs, a pair of bellows   8/0

In the Hall

A table board, 2 tressles, a cupboard, 2 chairs   6/-

In the Kitchen

4 water leads   20/-
2 leads, a brass pan   10/-
Item: 2 kenners, 3 kynmels, 2 vats, 3 pails, 6 barrels   6/6

In Naperie

7 pairs of sheets   23/4
5 coarse pairs of sheets   10/-
Item: 6 tablecloths, 6 towels, 7 tablet napkins   14/6
Item: 6 silver spoons   12/-
Item: 2 pillowbers   1/8
A pestle   5/-

His Wearing Apparel

     1 gown, a chamber jacket, a doublet of Worsted

     2 coats, 2 pairs of hose, 2 shirts, a cap   30/-

Debts (he) owed at the time of his death

     First a legacy debt to his daughter, Alice   £10

     Also to HENRY PLUMBER for a load   10/-

     To JOHN BISHOP for half a quarter of Malt   6/8

     Also Already to LAWRENCE GILBERT

     For 20 strikes of wheat   20/-

     Also to MARGARET BISCOOP   4/-

     Also for a quarter's rent   11/8

     Also to the vicar for his mortuary   3/4

Debts due to him at the hour of his death

     Of Master Busbie's executors   23/4

     Also of Walter Rymyll   10/-

     Also of John Hawkes   15/-

The whole sum, his debts paid   £19.6s.0d

FLIGHT SQUADRON LEADER ALAN GOODY, Retired. Landlord of THE GEORGE HOTEL 1960/70

Flight Squadron Leader Alan Goody (Retired) was the Landlord of The George Hotel, Lower Brailes. Pictured with him is his wife, The Rev Horace Wright and the Rev Allistaire Burnet, Methodist Minister of Brailes. Pictured in The George Hotel at this the first Harvest Home Service held at the local public house, circa 1960, the first year of Alan's ten years that he was landlord of this popular pub, 1960 until 1970. The HOOK NORTON ALE certainly loosened the tongues of many of the customers, who turned out to support this event. Produce and fruit sent along and brought in by Alan's customers was, after the service, donated to The Ellen Badger Hospital. It became an annual event, each succeeding vicar gladly fell in with the wishes of his flock, who, if not regular attendants at his church, certainly rose to the occasion at this local service.

Among those known on these photographs are the following:
Mrs L Gleed, George Howse, Fred Field, Jack Mumford, Jack Cummings,
Harry Burrows, Gilbert Hartwell, Jack Adams (Whichford), Albert Brain.

JACK BURY of ALMEADOW FARM became well-known for miles around, South Warwickshire in particular. The attraction was his coach, given that name, but in its younger days you would have been more likely to have seen a party of men carrying guns. It was an estate vehicle used to transport the invited guns to the chosen spots when the beaters had go to their appointed places, their job was to drive pheasant or partridges towards the guns ready and waiting to shoot as many of them as possible. The picture above tells us another story for Jack and his coach had been hired for a special occasion. He was accompanied by his son, John, and Mr Alan Goody, seated on top of the coach, Geoffrey Clifton and David Clemons with their coaching horns, both members of Brailes Brass Band. They were taking MISS VALERIE PETTIT to Cherington Church, where she was going to wed LEONARD JARRETT of Cherington. Valerie, a land girl, worked for the GASSON BROTHERS at MARSH FARM 1939/45 war years. Leonard, unknown to his future wife, had booked Jack for this particular day in her life, an occasion which happened some 60 years ago. Nice to see these happenings recorded in memory lane, which these pictorial histories are. Photographs by R E George, Moreton-in-Marsh, Glos. 10th September 1960.

Top: Jack Bury's coach at one of the local flower shows or carnival with Albert Rymel, an interest onlooker.

Bottom: The coach most likely going to participate in the Shipston Carnival. They won first prize on at least two occasions at this Carnival. No problem in getting passengers. At one Shipston Carnival GERALD COTTRELL played the part of Dick Turpin.

The house above is now known as BRAILES HOUSE, but going back in time an interesting family owned it, The Baker Family. Their names can be seen on tombstones in close proximity to the south port of St George's Church. They were farming land at Sutton-under-Brailes, and William Baker, the elder, was farming NEW HOUSE FARM, now owned by Mr Tom Taylor. In 1868 H J Sheldon, owner of the Manor of Brailes, sold New House Farm to ROBERT GARRETT. William Baker had moved to Brailes House across the road from the George Hotel, having the church of St George as a background. The Baker family were also farming FAMINGTON FARM in the late 1830's. They were listed as the owners of this farm in the 1841 Census. Stephen Stanbige was tenant at a rent of £35.00 per annum. Having put the larger half of Brailes Manor on the market in 1868, Henry James Sheldon got little response, selling, as previously mentioned, NEW HOUSE FARM. Shortly after William Baker purchased privately BRAILES HILL FARM and also GROVE END FARM, owning land from the parish of Barcheston and Cherington, the whole of Brailes Hill, and Grove End Farm, as well as renting land in Lower Brailes. JOHN BAKER, William's son, married the daughter of Doctor Cawley. The married couple were living at Grove End Farm, they had no issue. John Baker died prior to his wife and by his Will she inherited all the property owned by the late Baker family. At her death this property was inherited by Mrs Baker. The younger brother, William Wilkes Cawley inherited Brailes Hill and Grove End Farms, 1893/94. Prior to this he had been a London Barrister.

Above: Portraits of William Baker, the elder, and his wife. After the death of their son, John, their niece, Miss Gurney, was left Brailes House in John's wife's Will. The second son of Doctor Cawley at that time was living out in America. Miss Gurney was a benefactor to the village. She gave an Invalid

Carriage for the use of the elderly and sick in the Parish of Brailes and gave a complete set of New Uniforms for the Village Band.

Left: William Baker's mother.

8

Below: Portraits of JOHN BAKER as a teenager and a portrait of his wife, daughter of Doctor Cawley.

Above the Altar in Brailes Church you can see some plaques to note people of the village. Among the names are those of WILLIAM BAKER and of his wife, ELIZABETH BAKER. Attwoods and the Wincote's of Brailes and Whichford are there. The Wincote Tombs, however, are in Whichford churchyard.

In Memory of
ISABELLA ATTWOOD.
who died February 17. 1878.
Aged 82 Years.

In Memory of
WILLIAM BAKER.
Churchwarden. A.D. 1820-1862.
who died May 1. 1862.
Aged 82 Years.

In Memory of
ELIZABETH BAKER.
who died June 13. 1868.
Aged 89 Years.

Above: Is the Invalid Carriage given to the Parish Council by MISS EMMA GURNEY. It was later mistakenly sold to the SHAKESPEARE THEATRE IN STRATFORD. The Theatre Company had had the chair restored, but, when approached by the Council and had had the mistake explained, the

chair was returned to St George's Church on the understanding that if at anytime the Theatre needed a chair for any of its plays etc, they could have the loan of it. This was agreed to and so everyone was happy.

The last Brailes person to use the Invalid Chair was Mr Joseph Green of Sheep Street, Lower Brailes. Pictured with him in the chair are SUSAN CUMMINGS, DAVID EDWARDS, and ALFRED W O O D W A R D . C i r c a 1947/1948.

THE ROSE AND CROWN INN 1808. The Rose & Crown Inn, then PARK VIEW, and finally BLENHEIM HOUSE. The last owner, Mr Arnold Deller. The owner in 1808 was Thomas Cockbill, a Quaker whose family had been resident at Brailes form the mid-17th Century. He also owned the neighbouring property, IVY HOUSE. Thomas Cockbill employed an Innkeeper, named THOMAS RAINBOW. Thomas Cockbill sold the property in 1808 to a RICHARD JEFFERIES and he remained owner until 1816, and so long after that day as any principal money remains due under this Mortgage TO PAY interest by equal half-yearly payments on.

The 2 April and 22 October. And this Indenture also witnesseth that JOHN SPENCER as beneficial owner hereby conveys unto JOHN FOX a messuage or tenement at ASTON in the Parish of Bampton, Oxfordshire. And the adjoining tenement of 30 poles on the west side by the Rickyard formerly owned by John Henwood on the east. By the backside, formerly owned by Henry Hanks on the south, by the said orchard of John Henwood north, the said messuage was formerly owned by Elizabeth and Ann Clinch, then of William Townsend.

Reverend William Townsend and aunt, Barbara Townsend, and a messuage cottage with outbuildings etc. standing in Lower Brailes, Warwickshire, in the occupation of WILLIAM GODSON (Glover). Then of William Hands and since of Temperance Upton and now of JOHN SPENCER. JAMES UPTON (Deceased) purchased from Richard Godson of SWERFORD, Oxfordshire. Dates 16th and 17th August 1816. Conveyed and assured by Richard Godson and others to the use of James Upton, his heirs and assigns for ever. Also a piece or parcel of land or ground as stated, containing 480 square feet called and known as THE ROSE & CROWN INN, Lower Brailes.

WILLIAM HANDS and MRS HANDS. To be conveyed to JOHN SPENCER or his heirs provided the sum of £150.00 with interest has been paid, and that John Spencer or his heirs assure the property against damage or fire in the sum of £150.00 in the SUN FIRE OFFICE or some other insurance, and the receipt for covering premium payable in respect. Signed John Spencer. In the presence of William H Hall, Solicitor, Bampton, Oxfordshire.

Particulars of Mortgage 4th May 1901. Mr John Spencer to Mr John Fox, secure the sum of £150.00.

Inscribed on this deed in pencil, now mortgaged to Messrs GILLETT by transfer 15th July 1902..

A Conveyance dated 25th November 1852.

THE ROSE & CROWN INN. Being the LAST WILL and Testament of JAMES UPTON, Innholder, Brailes.

Robert Mansell of Brailes of the first part. JOHN GILLETTE of Brailes and Samuel Coleman of Shipston-on-Stour of the second part, Richard Davis of BRAILES (Draper) of the third part. Temperance Upton, Widow, and Mary Upton, spinster, both of Brailes of the fourth part, RICHARD WILKES (Farmer) of Sibford of the fifth part. Temperance Upton, widow of Thomas Upton labourer of Brailes.

INDENTURE 26th November 1852 BETWEEN John Spencer of Brailes and Richard Wilkes (Farmer) of Sibford.

JOHN SPENCER of the first part, RICHARD WILKES of the second part, FREDERICK HANCOCK of the third part. The for valuable property formerly in the hands of WILLIAM GODSON (GLOVER) of Brailes, since of WILLIAM HANDS, and now of TEMPERANCE UPTON. The previous schedule referred to an Indenture of FEOFFMENT, 1st January 1808 BETWEEN WILLIAM SHELDON of Grays Inn, Middlesex of the first part, JAMES UPTON aforesaid Innholder of Lower Brailes and JAMES SALISBURY FINDON of Shipston on Stour, Worcestershire, gentlemen of the second part.

INDENTURE: Lease made 16th August 1816.

INDENTURE Release made 17th August 1816.

BETWEEN RICHARD GODSON of Swerford (Yeoman) Co, Oxford. Therein further described of the one part and the said James Upton of Lower Brailes of the other part.

INDENTURE OF CONVEYANCE 26th November 1852 of the freehold premises known as The Rose & Crown Inn, Lower Brailes, Mr Richard Wilkes to Mr John Spencer.

MORTGAGE of a Cottage or dwelling house (Ivy Cottage) made 11th November 1858 situate in Lower Brailes. For the sum of £100.00 and interest Between MR DANIEL FIELD and another (Mary Field) to Mr Thomas Spencer.

CONVEYANCE 7th September 1863 of a freehold cottage and premises at Lower Brailes Between Mr Thomas Spicer, Mr Daniel Field, and Mrs Mary Field. To Mr John Spencer the sum of £100.00. Mr John Spencer received £100.00, Mr Daniel Field £50.00. Witness Mr Fred Hancock.

INDENTURE 22nd October 1887 BETWEEN Mr John Spencer of Cole, Nr Bampton, Oxfordshire and Mr John Fox, the receipt of which John Spencer acknowledges.

JOHN SPENCER covenants with JOHN FOX to pay him the 22nd April next the sum of £150.00 with interest. In the meantime after the rate of £4.10s per annum.

ELIZABETH WILKES nee ELIZABETH RICHARDSON in her Will she had named her nephew, RICHARD GODSON, of Swerford County of Oxford, JAMES UPTON, innkeeper, Lower Brailes. (James Upton had succeeded Thomas Rainbow as innkeeper at The Rose & Crown Inn, Lower Brailes). RICHARD GODSON or jointly with JAMES UPTON The Rose & Crown Inn at Lower Brailes was purchased for £50.00.

LEASE dated 11th October 1839 BETWEEN WILLIAM BAKER and SAMUEL GIBBS both of Brailes of the one part, SAMUEL FIELD (Grocer) of Brailes of the other part.

RELEASE: Of a Cottage and premises adjoining the Rose & Crown Inn (Ivy Cottage):

BETWEEN; WILLIAM BAKER of Brailes of the one part, SAMUEL GIBBS of Brailes of the second part, SAMUEL FIELD of Brailes of the third part, FREDERICK FRANCIS FINDON of Shipston-on-Stour of the fourth part.

THIS RELEASE relates to the LAST WILL and TESTAMENT of Richard Jefferies.

HIS BENEFICIARIES were RICHARD SUMMER, son of Elizabeth Summer £10.00, to the niece of ANN POTTER £10.00, to the three nephews of Richard Jefferies, Richard, Phillip, and John Jefferies each £10.00, to Hannah Cox, daughter of Ezroazs Cox, Taylor, £5.00.

INDENTURE dated 1st February 1906 BETWEEN JOHN SPENCER of Darlingscott (Farmer), Worcestershire of the one part, and of Phyllis, wife of John Spencer the younger, draper, of Shipston-on-Stour, Worcestershire of the other part.

WHEREAS the said John Spencer is seized of or entitled to the hereditaments hereinafter firstly described for an estate in fee simple in possession free from incumbrances and of or to the hereditaments hereinafter secondly described for a like estate in possession subject only to a Mortgage.

TRANSFERRED to the said Phyllis Spencer by an Indenture made 9th November 1905 whereon the sum of £174.13s.7d is now owing to the said Phyllis Spencer as part of her separate estate and WHEREAS the said John Spencer has agreed to sell the hereditaments to the said Phyllis Spencer at the price of £287.10s. And it has been said the Mortgage debt of £174.13s.7d be retained by Phyllis Spencer out of the purchase money.

Now this Indenture WITNESSETH that in consideration of the sum of £174.13s.7d RETAINED by the said Phyllis Spencer in full satisfaction of the said Mortgage Security (AND which last mentioned sum of £112.16s.5d, making with the sum of £174.13s.7d retained as aforesaid the purchase price of £287.10s, the said JOHN SPENCER hereby acknowledges)

The said John Spencer as beneficial owner, HEREBY CONVEYS unto Phyllis Spencer firstly ALL THAT cottage or tenement with the garden and premises thereto belonging, situate in the Parish of Lower Brailes, Warwickshire FORMERLY in the occupation of Thomas Rainbow, then Richard Jefferies, next of John Baily, since of Daniel Field, and now of Miss Matthews AND which said Cottage or Tenement and Premises formerly called "JUTSES" and secondly all that messuage or tenement, outhouses, edifices, and buildings with the yards, gardens, and backsides thereunto belonging situate at Lower Brailes Co Warwick.

Formerly occupied by William Godson (Glover) afterwards William Hands, then of Temperance Upton, and now of Robert Timms, also all that piece of land adjoining, containing 480 square feet, be the same as that adjoining The Rose & Crown Inn, Lower Brailes to hold the same unto and for the use of Phyllis Spencer for her separate use in fee simple. The hereditaments hereafter described freed and discharged from all equity and redemption subsisting therein under the said Indenture, 9th November 1905.

In witness whereof the said parties have set their hands and seals the day and year first above written.

Signed JOHN SPENCER

In the presence of H F Bennett, solicitor, Banbury

July 15th 1902, Mr John Fox and Mr John Spencer to Messrs Gillett and Company.

TRANSFER OF MORTGAGE (Written in Pencil on this Indenture).

Retrieved by Phyllis Spencer, wife of John Spencer the younger (Draper) of Shipston-on-Stour. Sum of £174.13s.7d. November 9th 1905.

Signatures Allen Charles E Gillett, John P Gillett, William Charles Braithwaite.

9

John Spencer to Mrs Phyllis Spencer.

In 1920 Mrs Phyllis Spencer sold The Rose & Crown Inn to Mr Ernest Bayliss, who lived there until 1934/5, the property was left to William Edward Bayliss after the death of Elizabeth Mary Bayliss, widow, on the 19th May 1935 at her home in High Street, Bloxham. W E Bayliss was administrator. He was left The Rose & Crown Inn, renamed Park View, and sold this property to Mr Arnold Deller, the elder, for £489.7s.10d. Arnold senior renamed the house and called it BLENHEIM HOUSE. He was an acting Fire Warden during the 1939/45 war years, but he could not stop the government from pulling down the IRON RAILINGS and gate posts and gate despite his protests. After his parents died, ARNOLD DELLER the younger became its owner, better known as Sandy Deller. He served his National Service with the Royal Air Force 1946-1949 and after he returned home he got married. After his wife's death Sandy decided in 1994 to erect iron railings, gate post, and gate to make the house look more like its old self.

The adjoining property "JUTSES" had been renamed IVY COTTAGE, which had been bought by Mrs Allen in 1920, later Ivy House was sold to Miss Ada Mary Biggs, initially she had been teaching at the Roman Catholic School in Banbury, but later moved to Ivy Cottage and taught at St Margaret's Roman Catholic School in Friars Lane, Lower Brailes. In 1994 Wilfred Locke was living in Ivy Cottage. He had worked for Cecil Righton as a car mechanic and later went to work at THE FORGE GARAGE for Douglas Cummings then for Doug's son-in-law, Mr Ian Haycock.

Top: Opposite The George Hotel from the eastern end, a butcher's shop owned by Mrs Lynes, and later by her son-in-law, Mr Jack Crook, and finally his daughter, Joan. Cottage in the centre of the row was where Mrs Brown used to live, one of the Edwardian villagers. The bottom view shows Mr Harry Hibberd with his donkey and cart. The butcher's shop has had a facelift, now having a coat of white paint on the shop front, and today a hairdressing salon. At the western end Joseph Boyce's bakery, afterwards run by his son.

ELLIOTT STORE, quite a small shop to begin with showing Mr and Mrs Elliott in the doorway. The trap was what he delivered orders with about the village. Larger windows and other changes including a branch of THE LONDON CITY and MIDLAND BANK. The piece of ground behind the iron railings left of the shop entrance Mr Elliott rented from Henry James Sheldon for 3d per annum. Some of his goods were displayed on these railings.

THE NOTICE BOARD was on the wall of THE POLICE STATION, Eborall, Taylor, Charlie Thomson, Bob Baldwin. Then it was converted by MISS THACKWELL, who had moved form THE PARK, Lower Brailes, into Brailes Post Office. The Village Stores where Mr Elliott traded acts as today's Post Office. Just below the archway with twin doors was the Lower Brailes Post Office. THOMAS PICKERING was the Post Master seen standing outside the building along with his wife, maybe some of his customers.

Above shows the row of three cottages, which ran from the Post Office down to The Rose & Crown Inn. Thatched roofs. Occupiers in the 1930's were Mr and Mrs Harry Hibberd senior, the Misses Standeven, and in the third was Mrs Emma Douglas, daughter of Harry Hibberd two doors away, and how the cottages looked after the thatch was taken off in either 1934 or 1935. Two of the cottages you can see were converted into one, and the slates were a great improvement.

The above photograph of the Bridge at Lower Brailes was taken from outside Blenheim House. It shows the bridge and the bend beyond to perfection for it was always looked upon as the boundary between Lower and Upper Brailes, for the road from the bend was devoid of houses or buildings of any description. The first to appear was NOOK FARMHOUSE, built by the ATTWOOD family in the mid-19th Century, then in later years the appearance of houses everywhere. I do not know the year the bridge was built. Most like in the 17th Century. 1690 was when the road became recognised, so that may perhaps coincide with the bridge. A FORD was at one time in use in that area long before the stone wall was built by the Attwoods firm of builders for the Sheldon family, and the only feasible place for the ford would have been in the now enclosed part of the Brailes House grounds, just below the sluice, recognised for it has a waterfall running down a set of steps. Between that and the bridge a hardish bottom can be seen during the summer, a low bank almost opposite SHEEP STREET, which was the recognised main trackway running through Lower Brailes in the 15th Century.

Above a picture of the GIRLS' SCHOOL at Lower Brailes situated at the western end of St George's Church. Something like 40 girls were taught at this school. Then in 1856 THE NEW SCHOOLS were under construction. Mrs Sheldon laid the foundation stone. Below is a picture of what the schools, Girls and Infants, would look like on completion. Drawn by the Architect, Mr William Smith, son of the Rev Thomas Smith. In 1835 Isabella Attwood was teacher at the Girls' school. Winifred Pickering taught the infants.

The land in Sheep Street was given by Henry James Sheldon. The Rev Thomas Smith was the person who began the fundraising. The Sheldons, as well as giving the land, and Mrs Sheldon laying the foundation stone, gave £80.00 to the fund. Other notable families also gave similar amounts. Total cost of building the two schools and a house for a teacher was almost £1,000.00, a tidy sum in those days. Headmaster at the Church of England School in my school days was Mr John Morris, and then in 1934 Mr Hector Baden Ward was appointed as Head Teacher.

ST MARGARET'S ROMAN CATHOLIC SCHOOL was founded by Father Duckett in 1823 and after his death in 1864 the school was transferred to a cottage in Friars Lane, Lower Brailes. This cottage, along with others, were destroyed by fire, and the owner, LADY BEDINGFIELD, had what remained of the cottage converted into a SCHOOL ROOM. This old school room has since been converted into a cottage.

Brailes School children. The photograph was taken in 1890. None of the children have been recognised. If I had begun researching some 30 to 40 years earlier I might have been more successful.

Below Brailes Infant class taken in 1910. At least one I know, the boy sitting between two girls in the front is Charles Field of Lower Brailes.

A group of Brailes Children attending the school in Sheep Street, named changed to School Lane after the New School had been built. 1912/1913.

From Left to right back row: Ernest Bradley, killed on Gallow Hill after crashing into a Midland Red Bus on his motorcycle, Elvet Davis, Harvey Davis, Raymond Bayliss, emigrated to Canada, Owen Warmington, John Wakeham, Harold Hibberd, went to live in Coventry, H W C Papworth, his son was killed in the 1914/18 war.

Centre row: William Burrows, Jack Moulder, Gladys Davis, Lil Roberts, Lowrie Clay, Joyce Clay, Phyllis Harris.

Front Row: Harold Chilton, Amos Bryan, May Timms, May Field, Hilda Austin, Edith Hitchman of Winderton, Mildred Sparks, Nellie Field, Tom Chilton.

Brailes C of E School 1916/17.

Left to right: Bill Burrows, James Boyce, Harold Hibberd, Mark Taylor, Stan Taylor, Jim Steel, Jack Moulder, and Austin Haycock.

Centre Row: Ruby Bayliss, Florence Hall, Amos Bryan, Tom Chilton, Harold Chilton, Harold Clifton, Emma Wakeham, Esther Parker, Emma Hawtin.

Front Row: Evelyn Hall, Joan Manders, Joyce Clay, Connie Clay, Hilda Parsons, Lillian Roberts, Gladys Davis, Hilda Austin.

Two girls standing in front of H W C Papworth, headmaster, were Ina Hitchman and May Field.

Two girls on the left: May Timms and Nancy Field.

Top and Bottom show pupils at the C of E School at Lower Brailes during the 1930's. Top shows Mr John Morris, Headmaster, on the right. Bottom shows Mrs Pedley on the right. She was often left in charge when the Headmasters had to attend some meeting in Warwick. On one occasion, thinking she was a soft touch, we began playing around and found out to our sorrow when she punished us with having to learn the 119 Psalm and recite it to her before gaining our freedom.

These two photographs are of the school groups of the 1920's. The actual year of the top one is unknown, but the bottom picture is of the pupils in 1928. Names of both groups are known and will be found on a full list of names for all six pictures. The headmaster, although not shown, would have been Mr John Morris with Mrs Pedley teacher of the infants.

Pupils' names in the school group. Top Page 104 - Back row, left to right: John Cummings, Percy Butler, Albert Locke, Jack Phillips, Reginald Spicer, Harold Chilton, Oliver Warmington, UK, Kenneth Warmington. Centre: Gladys Box, UK, Joyce Clay, Winnie Durham, Freda Harris, May Timms, Rosie Beck. Headmaster: Mr John Morris.
2nd Row: UK, UK, Gladys Hawtin, Lucy Hawton, UK, Ida Woodward. Front: James Boyce, Fred Hitchman, UK, Peter Drinkwater, Jack Mumford, Marshall Sharp, Joseph Harris, UK.

Bottom of Page 104.
Left to right: Norman Green, Marshall Sharp, Jack Mumford, Albert Locke, Alwyn Davis, Reginald Hitchman, UK. Clarks Pickering, Douglas Cummings. Centre: Kenneth Chilton, Cecil Hibberd, Thomas Chilton, Thomas Woodward, UK, Eric Cummings, Mabel Chilton, UK, UK; Teacher: Mrs Pedley. Front: Lucy Hawtin, Ida Woodward, UK, UK, UK, UK, Hilda Hitchman, UK, James Boyce, Mary Mumford, UK.

Top of Page 105.
Left to right: Norman Green, Tom Boyce, UK, Marshall Sharp, John Boyce, George Wheeler, Harry Burrows, Douglas Hibberd. Centre: Muffy Chinnor, Rosy Durham, Margaret Green, Ada Walker, Mary Mumford, Nancy Chilton, Joyce Twist, Better Miller. Front: William Manley, Harry Betteridge, Thomas Woodward, Maurice Warmington, Gordon Drinkwater, Douglas Durrant, Eric Cummings, Leslie Charnock.

Bottom of Page 105.
Left to right: Alfred Woodward, Leslie Parker, Henry Warmington, Marshall Green, Peter Mumford, John Clemons, Albert Hibberd, Sidney Hibberd, Walter Cummings, Albert Moulder, Charles Cuthbert, John Hawtin, Harry Hibberd. Centre: Eileen Parker, Edna Parker, Barbara Pickering, Joan Chinnor, Peggy Craven, Hilda Batchelor, Phyllis Hibberd, Betty Boyce, Henrietta Douglas, Gertie Hall, Edna Sumners, Rosie Parker. Front: Dorothy Clemons, Daisy Woodward, Margaret Craven, Helen Sumners, John Sumners, Clemence Hibberd, Olive Charnock.

Top and Bottom: Top is a photograph of the 5th and 6th Form Boys and Girls 1934. Bottom: The pupils in the 1940's Boys and Girls.
Top picture shows the pupils at the time Mr Hector Baden Ward was headmaster.
Bottom picture shows Mrs F N Gill in charge of the class in 1955/56.

Names of the pupils in 1933/34.

Forms 5 and 6, given from left to right. Back Row - Barbara Pickering, Gwennie Gilkes, Dorothy Chilton, John Clemons, William Manley, Maurice Warmington, Douglas Durrant.

3rd - Peggy Craven, Muffy Chinnor, Joyce Twist, Ada Shepherd, Hilda Batchelor, Ken Wheeler, Tom Boyce, Douglas Hibberd, Marshall Green, Albert Moulder.

2nd - Doris Shepherd, Dorothy Clemons, Olive Charnock, Gertie Hall, Betty Boyce, Henry Warmington, Walter Cummings, Phyllis Hibberd, Joan Chinnor, Betty Miller.

Front - John Hawtin, Alfred Woodward, Leslie Parker, Sidney Hibberd.

BRAILES COUNCIL SCHOOL 1955/56

Back row - John Box, Leslie Gleed, Kenneth Bradley, Eric Smith, Eddy Betteridge, Neville Gleed, Richard Ratcliffe. Teacher: Mrs F N Gill.

3rd - Ivor Betteridge, Kathleen Webb, Janet Warmington, UK, ? Hall, UK, UK, Colin Shurmer.

2nd - Margaret Baldwin, Violet Warmington, Jennifer Ratcliffe, Monica Field, UK, ? Chilton, Joan Sumners.

Front - Michael Mumford, Gordon Rogers, Tony Betteridge.

The pupils who attended the Roman Catholic School, ST MARGARET'S in Friars Lane.

Back, left to right - Robert Crook, Harold Bryan, Alice Bryan.

Centre - Annie Bryan, Joan Crook, Alec Warmington, Agnes Bryan, Miss Trevor, Connie Bryan.

Front - Harry Bryan, John Bryan, Ada Walker, Winnie Bryan, Mary Walker.

The Bryan Families were the children of Mr John Bryan. They lived in Friars Lane. The other family were the children of Mr James Bryan. They lived in the old Thatched Houses on the left of the footpath, which went into the Park and then finally they lived in the end cottage of the first six council houses to be built in The Park.

The large Elm Trees which once graced The Park and the nearby Village Green were all lost when they were attacked by Dutch Elm Disease.

BRAYLES GRAMME SCHOLE or as later named, THE OLD BOYS SCHOOL. Headmaster and mistresses who taught at this Old School over the course of the years are as follows: E Winchester 1888-1891, T E Paine 1890's-1900, W FORD 1900, substituted during an eight-week illness by Mr Oakes 1900-1902, J Brade and wife. The infant school in the house close to the west end of St George's Church where at one time Mr Fred Gander quoted up to 70 of them, wife was the infant teacher. J B Jones 1902-1903, two monitors H Wheatley and S Mumford 1903 to 1923, H W C Papworth, assistant Arthur Pickering, other assistants who followed Arthur were Bernard Shiel, Percy Thomson, Alfred Smart, Alice Dane, who married Alwyn Papworth, son of H W C Papworth 1903 to 1923, John Morris 1923 to 1934, Hector Baden Ward, 1934 to 1943, Mrs B Findlay 1944 to 1947, Mrs F Meyer and Mrs F N Gill 1947 to 1955 to 1968. After the latter year, 1968, senior pupils were sent to Shipston on Stour High School.

MAY DAY Celebrations at Brailes. No effort to put on a good performance on the 1st May. These two scenes are from the day's events in 1905. In the 1930's Harold Matthews was taking bus loads of people from Brailes to see the celebrations at Shipston-on-Stour. An all day event. Brailes may have been as attractive for 1st May was a National Event, and as these

THE MAY POLE   BRAILES

pictures show was enjoyed by many in the school playground in SHEEP STREET. The second event was held in 1906 and in that year Miss Emma Harriet Mumford born in 1894, was the 12-year-old May Queen. She left school in 1906, at the age of 12 years to work as an assistant cook in Shipston-on-Stour. Her mother worked for Doctor Finlay, and that perhaps explains why Mother Harriet was Brailes's midwife and

MAY-DAY BRAILES - 1906

MAY-DAY BRAILES - 1906

laid out the Dead of Brailes. Her midwifery was perhaps picked up through working for the good doctor, who died at the bedside of a patient he was attending, having suffered a massive heart attack. Harriet lived to be 100 years and six months. Her daughter Emma was 94 in 1988.

THE MAYPOLE   BRAILES

Two more scenes of May Day events. Well attended as you can see. Days when self-entertainment was the well-known thing. More enjoyment attained this way then for any large gathering, with few days holiday, everyone was welcomed and, as these scenes show, fully enjoyed.

Top: The May Queen with her attendants, and the boys playing the part of her courtiers. Below the 1913 May Day event. Names of almost everyone in this photograph are known and so it will add to the pleasure of knowing, unlike the earlier ones, when perhaps I was fortunate enough to have spoken to someone who knew the story behind Harriet and Emma Mumford.

The May Day Celebrations in 1913 had a different outlook about it, for no maypole can be seen, just one boy with a May Garland. The two adults in the pictures were Miss Kate Woodward and Amy Steel, who may have already married George Field, for she had originated from the village of Willington, and George Field was roundsman for the Steel's carrier business. Amy was the daughter of the man who owned the business. Names in order as they appear on the photograph are Miss Kate Woodward and at the other end of the back row was Amy Steel, Bob Sharp with the May Garland, behind him Fred Field, Nellie Field, Kathleen Parker, Alice Baldwin, Fanny Warmington, Kate Hibberd, Vera Field, Alice Bryan, Wilfred Warmington, Annie Bryan, and John Baldwin. The May Queen was Miss Nancy Field, and her courtier was William Hancock. The boy and girl seated in the foreground were Bill Walker and May Field.

Sheep Street before mains water or flush toilets had come into people's lives, and the cottages are not telling a true story for since the 15th Century this street had been the main thoroughfare through the village, the road in use today had not been opened.

Many of the houses on the left-hand side as you go from off the main road had been burnt down. They were originally stone-built, and after the fire, when they were rebuilt, the back of the houses were rebuilt with stone, using the good stone that had been at the front. The front of the cottages as you can see were rebuilt with bricks, giving a false impression of their real age, years earlier than the bricks tell us.

Mr Frank Miller the elder with his family and relations. From the left: William Miller, son, Frank Miller senior, Father, Mary Ann wife, Frank Bryan Sutton-under-Brailes, wife Emma Bryan nee Miller. Seated grandmother, Fred Miller on the end, in front by his mother is Frank Miller, son. The Miller family have lived in Sheep Street for over 200 years, and Fred Miller's daughter, Betty, still owns the house this photograph was taken in front of.

Above: Some members of the Hibberd family taken in Sheep Street, Lower Brailes. Those known are - Back: Cecil, Father Frederick, Joan York. In front: Winnie York nee Hibberd, Mrs Agnes Lambert Hibberd, and Kate. Below: Mr Frederick Burroughs and Miss Kate Hibberd, later Fred's wife. Preparing to ride back to Coventry. They had ridden to Brailes the day previous. Other people on the picture are unknown. In front on top picture is Miss Joan York.

11

Above: Thomas Henry and Martha Woodward with their daughters, Sarah and Kate.

Below: Harry and Hannah Selina Woodward, Daughter, Mrs Daisy Edwards, David Edwards, Thomas Henry the younger, and Sydney and Ida Webb, son-in-law and daughter.

Mr Albert Summers on right with his father, mother, and sister and other members of his family. Pictured at his home in Honington. Albert married Miss Emma Hawtin and came to live in Sheep Street with his two daughters, Nancy and Joan.
Below: Ralph Welch talking to Leonard Townley in Sheep Street, while Christine Bryan is trying to get out of range of the camera.

Left: Joe and Betsy Green out in the garden at the rear of their home in Sheep Street. Below are their twin daughters Joan and Jean. How old they were at this stage in their life I do not know, but married and still living in Lower Brailes, the village they were born in. So many Brailes people have that privilege I am happy to say.

Left: Sergeant Norman Green R.E.M.E. Worcestershire Regt 1939/45. Called up in the second wave of The Militia. He was Lance Corporal when this picture was taken. Below: From left - Alfred Woodward, Marshall Green, Walter Cummings, three 18-year olds on Sunday Morning 3rd September 1939. We walked down the lane to hear war declared against Germany. Marshall and I were working on the farm and were put in a reserve occupation and served in the Home Guards, Dads Army. Later Walter was called up for Army Service and served R.A.S.C 1941-1945.

Left: Joyce Twist pictured with her pet dog. Was living with her grandmother, Mrs Bryan. This dog was not always as quiet, for one day it came out of the house, and several boys were kicking a ball about. Jack Mumford's cap came off, and the dog ran and picked it up and shook it like shaking a rate. The cap was rather tattered by the time he had finished with it.

Left: Picture of Amos Bryan's wedding. Brother, Bill, behind him, the best man, with Joyce the smaller of the two bridesmaids. Mrs Dickie Bryan, as she was known, lived in Sheep Street throughout my whole school days. I remember one Christmas going along to her home and sharing one or two of the goodies on the Christmas tree.

Miss Betty Miller of Sheep Street, Lower Brailes. Pictured with her nephew, John Bryan, of Sutton-under-Brailes. John's grandfather had married Betty's father's sister. I have recorded some of the families who lived in Sheep Street for virtually the whole of their life and some, sadly I have to say, are no longer with us. It jogged me into action again to get more of the history I have collected into book form for future generations, who will be living in this old town, reduced to the status of a village, for the old business which used to be around vanished. The new industrial estate at Brailes has replenished the job situation to some extent. More I hope will be said about them.

Page 43 - Post Building

Page 100 - Catholic School

Page 48

Page 52

The Park view in oils. Rev. Smith's Daughter, Maude - the youngest.

Thanks Rob T.

Page 125 - 'Ted' Claydon Hurdle Workshop

18636 PRIVATE EDWIN WALDRON CLAYDON
B COMPANY 3RD BATTALION SOMERSET LIGHT INFANTRY.
ATTESTED 11TH JULY 1917, MOBILIZED 14TH MAY 1918.
WOUNDED WITH 1ST BATTALION SOMERSET LIGHT
INFANTRY 24TH OCTOBER 1918, TRANSFERED T/O
ARMY RESERVE 25TH OCTOBER 1919

ALSO ENTITLED TO THE
1939-45 DEFENCE MEDAL
FOR SERVICE AS A PRIVATE
IN THE BRAMLES HOME
GUARD. HE NEVER CLAIMED
THE MEDAL.

Page 128 - Edward   Page 130 - His medals

Page 158 - William Manley (Insert Page 155)

Page 168 - Brayles House

Page 170 - Original '99' - ? - steps

Page 170 - Wood Bridge & '99' steps

Page 173 - Dry Sutton Brook - see text

Page 175 - Tin Mill handwheel & belt-drive pulley

Page 176a - Artists impression 'Tat' Taylor's Tin Mill - on Sutton Brook

12

Brailes House Estate Carpenter's Shop and Yard was the last place the Claydon family made hurdles and other things that were used on the farm. It was from this Carpenter's Shop that the things prepared beforehand were taken to Church End Farm, Maxstoke, Warwickshire, where a recording of Country Calendar was being filmed. Ted Claydon was on set for 13 minutes, for all he had to do was fit the prepared parts into a hurdle from the parts he had been filmed making at his local Carpenter's Shop. This was on 28th March 1953. The viewing public saw him, he split a head or shaft, the rest he assembled the ready-made parts. I once asked him what his weekly output of hurdles was, and he told me from pole to finished hurdle, two-to-three score hurdles a week. More will be seen and heard about the Claydon family in part two if everything goes to plan. Ted was pictured twice showing the finished hurdle. One you can see his niece with him, and this was in the yard. The other was taken with Fred Miller at which time they were standing in the Shop doorway. You can see Ted's bicycle leaning against the door, his only means of transport, for he never owned or drove a motor car. The art of hurdle making can be seen on the series of photographs, which follow these opening remarks.

1.William Claydon began his hurdle making business on College Green, Upper Brailes. His son, Edwin, began his career as hurdle maker after the 1914-18 war, sometime in 1919. The business was first started in the late 1880's.

2.Shaping the spars with a draw knife.

3.Splitting a willow pole out to length, for the making of them into hurdle heads.

4.Shaping the heads with a razor-sharp axe.

5.Drilling and cutting out the mortice in the hurdle heads into which the spars were fitted.

6.A picture of the completed hurdle head.

7.Edwin pictured with a selection of spars and heads, enough to make a five-spar hurdle.

8.Edwin making the hurdle heads where the mortice joint was cut. This ensured the spars were an equal distance apart.

9.Edwin assembling a five-spar hurdle. Hurdles at the Agricultural Shows where Edwin completed were always six-spar ones.

10.A smile of satisfaction on Edwin's face as he displays a completed five-spar hurdle with Mr Fred Miller.

11.The same old smile as Edwin is photographed with his niece in the Old Brailes House timber yard with another completed hurdle. Note the pile of wood shavings, these Edwin sold for 6d a bagful to the local housewives for fire lighting.

12.Edwin Claydon and his wife, Violet, photographed at an Agricultural Show close to Northampton where Edwin had gone to judge the hurdle-making contest in the late-1950's after his appearance on television on 28th March 1953. The above photographs illustrate what Edwin did at this televised event.

Top: Ted showing how to split a head or shaft and the different tools he used for each operation. Note the hand-made frame he used for splitting the willow poles on. Bottom picture shows some more of the tools he used.

Ted Claydon busy shaping one of the spars, which ran the length of a hurdle, using a draw knife, one of the tools of his trade. The shavings he made were sold for 6d a bag, no restriction on the size of the sack, they all cost 6d. He also used the shavings and wood no longer any use for his trade and had a nice fire going during the winter months.

Bottom picture shows Ted and his wife taking things easy after he had made a hurdle on television. I have mentioned this event in my opening remarks. They had no children and so Ted on his retirement left Brailes with another lost trade.

Left: Edwin Claydon shaping a shaft, note how high the chopping block was. Had it have been lower Ted, as he was known, would have ended up with an aching back by the end of the day. He usually prepared enough of each part of a hurdle in six's. This method was to ensure he made his weekly quota of hurdles, about two-to-three score in a week.

Ted served with the Somerset Regiment. 18636 Private Edwin Waldron Claydon 'B' Company 3rd Battalion, Somerset Light Infantry. Attested 11th July 1917. Mobilised 14th May 1918. His call up was delayed for a year for his brother was killed in action about the time he had attested. Wounded 24th October 1918, transferred to Army Reserve 25th October 1919.

18636 PRIVATE EDWIN WALDRON CLAYDON B COMPANY 3RD BATTALION SOMERSET LIGHT INFANTRY. ATTESTED 11TH JULY 1917, MOBILIZED 14TH MAY 1918. WOUNDED WITH 1ST BATTALION SOMERSET LIGHT INFANTRY 24TH OCTOBER 1918, TRANSFERED TO ARMY RESERVE 25TH OCTOBER 1919.

Top: Shows Ted drilling a header, note how he holds the drill, and using his chest to pressure the drill while he turns the drill using his left hand. Bottom shows him as a young man, taking things a little easy as he sits at the front of his home, GABLE END. I imagine this was prior to his war service.

Left: Ted Claydon standing in the doorway with a complete set of heads and rails to make a hurdle. Not much longer before he has a complete hurdle on display. He still has work to do on the heads, which was shown on the preceding photograph. The next pictures will show Ted doing the assembling of these heads and rails.

Below I have included a picture of Ted's military medals and the Cap Badge of the Somerset Light Infantry. The medals are the 1914/18 War Medal and the Defence Medal. Ted served with the Local Defence Volunteers. Later the name was changed to THE HOME GUARD. He was entitled to the 1939/45 Defence Medal, but never claimed it.

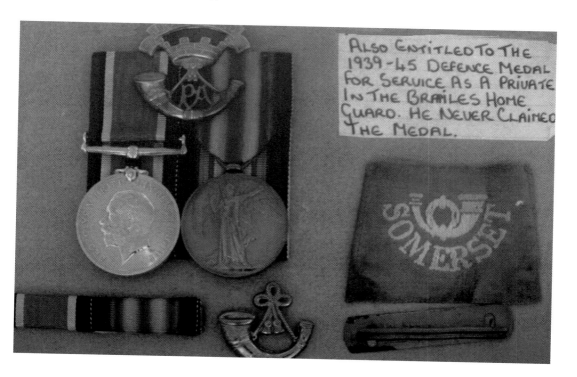

ALSO ENTITLED TO THE 1939-45 DEFENCE MEDAL FOR SERVICE AS A PRIVATE IN THE BRAMLES HOME GUARD. HE NEVER CLAIMED THE MEDAL.

Top: Ted laying out the hurdle, marking the head where he intends the rails to be, then repeat the process at the other end. Bottom you can see him fitting the rails into the heads and then to complete the hurdle he will fasten them firmly in place with some Blacksmith-made nails.

Top: Ted Claydon pictured with his niece displaying the completed hurdle. In the doorway of Ted's Carpenter's Shop you can see Ted and Mr Fred Miller showing another of Ted Claydon's Sheep Hurdles. The hurdles were used to make pens into which the Sheep were put to graze off the root crops planted for that purpose, but you seldom see this type of farming today.

Ted Claydon's work became scarcer as modern methods were introduced. Where Ted was making Wooden Cattle Cribs, manufacturers were turning out tubular metal cribs, which lasted longer and, produced in bulk, brought the prices down to a level Ted could not compete with. With Ted's demise at an early age of 61 years and having no children, another trade was lost to Brailes. Ted's wife lived on to the age of 81 years.

From ESTATE CARPENTER'S SHOP to A LUXURY BUNGALOW and given the name of HURDLES was what emerged after the shop was sold for £90,000 on 31st October 1988. A timber merchant had purchased the Miss Nelson estate, but all he was interested in was the standing timber. He felled all the trees and then sold the land and Brailes House at a knock-down price to Mr Basil Taylor, a sitting tenant on some of the land. Basil cleared the tree tops left by the timber merchant and sold them. Then after one wing was pulled down to make the house smaller and more saleable, he proceeded to apply and build bungalows and houses in the small coppices running from Blue Gates in both directions. Richard Neal, who had built the bungalow, found no-one to purchase it and so he lived there fore a number of years, but sold it eventually.

THE CRINKLE CRANKLE WALL as it is referred to may be amongst the lost places of Brailes Interest, for I have heard that Planning Permission is being asked to allow today's owner to convert and build more houses on the site. All the outhouses and stables at Brailes House have been converted into dwellings and so this, if granted, will make the Brailes House buildings to have completely disappeared. Originally built in the early-19th Century by the Sheldons, most likely Edward Ralph Charles Sheldon, born on 2nd March 1782. He was a staunch Church Warden at St George's Church, a Major of the Warwickshire Militia, Deputy Lieutenant of Warwick, a Justice of the Peace, and a Member of Parliament for South Warwickshire in 1835, but 12 months later on 11th June 1836, he died at the age of 54 years. The Crinkle Crankle Wall enclosed quite a large garden, and the high wall at the north, north-east side had grapes, peaches, apricots, plums, pears etc. Gooseberries, black and red currants, strawberries and other delicacies were growing in the garden with a few apple trees dotted in it. In the 1930's it could have been taken for the Garden of Eden. The school boys were often tempted to raid it, for a great deal of the fruit trees had survived. One evening, when I was living at Blackwell, L T C Rolt, who was living in Sibford telephoned me. He was researching the work of INIGO JONES and wanted to know what I could tell him about the Brailes House garden. I told him as much as I am saying now.

He replied "very interesting". It is obviously on lines of Inigo Jones's work, but not of this period. Today all you can see are a few scrub trees.

TRASHING BEANS AT DURNINGS BARN. Frank Vincent Webb after travelling the Thrashing Drum around South Warwickshire for countless years, at one accompanied by Mr Bert Gibbs of Ascot, then later with Cyril Bartlett. Frank finally purchased the Thrashing Drum and began travelling the Drum on his own. The land at Durnings Barn was rented by Mr Teddy Middleton from the Marquis of Northampton and today the Cottage, barn, and stables have all been knocked down, modern methods of Farming have

eliminated this method of thrashingand seldom, if ever, will you see it unless some proud collector will put on an exhibition at some agricultural show. The

first two pictures show Frank and Lucy Webb on the drum, Lucy cutting the bonds while Frank feeds the corn into the drum, Wilfred Warmington unloading the wagon, and at the rear of the drum Mr Middleton looking after the bags. As each sack fills up with corn he puts on an empty sack, ties the neck of the full sack, and then it gets loaded onto a trailer to be taken down to Rectory Farm in Lower Brailes.

The man on the empty wagon is unknown so is the young boy on the tractor, but the man with his hand on the front of the tractor is Alec Warmington. On the loaded trailer below are several boys, the man who had been unloading the wagon, Wilfred Warmington, and the dog, not to be left out. In the 1930's, with a recession still active, the only work for many of the local men virtually followed the Thrashing Drum from farm to farm. Seasonable work was about the only time they found employment, the rest of the time they had to report twice a week, to see if any jobs were to be had. Otherwise they would get about eight shillings unemployment pay.

Haymaking time on Chinslade Farm in South Warwickshire, where is that you may wonder? In the 1940's a different way of life prevailed, taking home the well-made hay. Not the picture I would have liked, but I hope my photographer will enhance the copy I have of a Pair of Shire Horses pulling a farm wagon with a hay loader behind, picking up the well-made hay and dropping it onto the wagon, where a man, not shown, would keep levelling it out until a well-loaded wagon would be taken to the rick yard by a Ford Tractor, and a tow bar made to attach to the shafts of the wagon. No bails in the 1940's. They came only for the rich farmer in their infancy, then with luck the hay could have been thrown from the wagon into an elevator. Prior to that laboriously fork-by-fork thrown onto a hay stack, which later would be thatched to keep out the rain.

With double summer time, the hay gathering could go on to 10.00 pm or later. Long days and late nights, you still reported for work at 7.00 am the following morning, best not to mention take-home pay. Chinslade Farm was off the road running from Sutton-under-Brailes through to Traitors Ford. The arrival of the farm tractor brought about the change we see in these two haymaking pictures. The first sign that horse-drawn transport had reached the end of the road.

Above: Miss Gwennie Gilkes driving home the heavily-laden wagon load of hay, with brother William standing on the tow bar. Below shows Miss Gwennie Gilkes with her uncle and aunt, Mr and Mrs Hemstock, sitting in the trap behind the pony who had been broken in to this type of work. A trip round the countryside in the fresh summer air, free from pollution, which today's modern machinery produces.

A typical scene in the 1930's when the Thrashing Drum and portable BURRILL STEAM ENGINE arrived outside the farmyard of Brailes Hill Farm, for from where the teams of horses pulling the drum and engine had been halted, they had to be pulled by these two teams and additional horses the 800 feet to the HILL BARN on top of BRAILES HILL. The accompanying pictures will illustrate the effort the teams were asked to produce.

The second picture shows that ten horses hitched in pairs were required to
pull the Thrashing Drum up into the field called Ashen Coppice, five of the
horses were then unhitched and the drum then continued on its way to the
Hill Barn. The five horses unhitched were then taken back to the main road
and hitched to the Burrill Steam Engine, a stationary one, used to drive the
drum, and for other uses. Many were found in Timber Yards, providing
power to drive the saws. The picture below shows the drum and portable
engine through Ashen Coppice. I would imagine the horses pulling the drum
had been rested while the others were taken to pull the engine up into Ashen
Coppice. They would be handy if the five horses got into any difficulties
while pulling the Burrill Engine. For the picture below shows all ten horses,
five of each of the pieces of machinery needed to thrash the corn stacked in
the Hill Barn. About half the horses would be used to pull them back down
hill to the main road. Mr Cox was farming Brailes Hill Farm in the 1930's,
and I know that he had a useful team of horses, but on this occasion a
neighbouring farm would provide the extra horses required for this one task.

A common sight at Gallows Hill Farm, when the farm machinery was being brought out to cultivate the land. This time it was the planting season, for amongst the machinery was a Horse Drawn Drill. The accompanying wagon etc. would have had the seed corn on board and maybe a set of harrows. This scene was about 1900, with Henry James Sheldon, a bankrupt at the time. The Estate was being run by Solicitors,

one example was perhaps a sign of his monetary problems, having tried unsuccessfully to sell off half the Manor of Brailes, which he owned in 1868. Again evidence was provided when on Wednesday, 17th September 1890, Henry James Sheldon sold his flock of 340 pedigree Shropshire Sheep he had been keeping on Gallows Hill Farm, among them many prize winners, for almost every show he entered his sheep in he was a winner. This failed to solve his difficulties for seven years later he put the remainder of the Brailes Manor Estate up for auction. Miss Nelson purchased the greater part of this Manorial Estate, 1.728 acres, and this part of the estate remained in her hands until her death in June or July, for the estate was sold off on 5th August 1920. If confirmation that he was in difficulties when the following picture was taken of the HARPER FAMILY of Oxhill professional Hay tiers, such a large estate must have been difficult to make profit on, for the cost of repair work to properties were greater than the income from them. The two former pictures Circa 1900 would have been about the time that Mr Thomas Quarterly was tenant farmer.

45

This Barrow and Stewart Portable Steam Engine belonged to JOHN HEMMINGS of Brailes, the elder and his two sons, John the younger and Richard Hemmings. Built in Banbury circa 1870.

From evidence I have found out that it was purchased new by John Hemmings of Brailes. The photographs I have were taken at the time of the BURY family of GREAT TEW 1956/57. This family had purchased the Barrow and Stewart engine from William Burrows, Broadmoor Lodge, Wolford. Its serial number was No.542. Dimensions: Overall length eight-feet-six inches, height to top of flywheel seven-feet-six inches, the flywheel three-feet-eleven inches, Diameter X four feet in width. Cylinder Bore five-and-a-half inches, stroke nine inches, working pressure 60 PSI.

The boiler is lagged in varnished mahogany without sheet cladding. The big end is now of the marine-type not the strap and wedge type. A small bypass valve and tap to the feed pump has been added. Pictured on the previous page at an engine rally at ALTON TOWERS circa 1960's, it then disappeared for some 25 years and was found by DAVID PLANT in 1987 as a heap of scrap and after taking it home he restored the engine. The sale was at Thruxton. He then sold it to its present-day holder, who brought it back to Brailes and put it on exhibition with a saw it had used to originally provide power for in the hands of MR KENNETH DURHAM, the engine owner. MR HAMISH ORR EWING resisted all efforts to purchase it.

Above: It's first home from where it was sold Circa 1947 to William Burrows. The yard pictured above belonged to the GODSON and HEMMING families for generations. After Richard Hemmings's death, without issue, the business was run for his widow, Mrs Laura Hemmings, nee Godson, by the young man Richard had apprenticed, Mr Raymond Locke. He finally purchased the business from Mrs Hemmings and, although the firm of Locke & Son are no longer wheelwrights or carriers, they do run the undertakers business, having enlarged and had built a CHAPEL OF REST on CAUTION CORNER, UPPER BRAILES.

CYDER MAKING was a thriving business in season at Brailes as early as the 17th Century confirmed by this extract from the Parish Register. Robert, the sonne of Valentine Holyfield a Chapman was buried in 1641. He was slayne by the Crab Mill of John Bishop in Over Brayles. John Bishop's Crab Mill stood on the hill top to the north-west of Castle Hill and has always been referred to as Bishops Castle. It's correct name is The Hangings, but through the courtesy of The Birmingham Mail, who gave me permission to use the photographs they had taken, I am able to give you the updated version of Cyder Making at Over Brailes circa 1960's. The cider press is centuries old. The pulper of a later date. This is driven by a 3hp Donkey Engine, the earliest known owners of this Cyder Press were members of The Godson family, Richard Godson was first, but after being left a vested interest in The Rose & Crown Inn at Lower Brailes 1816, he left it to Charles Godson, from him to William Decimus Godson, then on to Richard Hemmings, and in the 1960's Raymond Locke became owner. On the rare occasions it is used today, it is a combination of Raymond and John Clemons.

The Apple Pulper is housed in a wooden frame, a round metal drum with protruding spikes on it, the apples are put into a wooden trough, the pulper is driven at high speed by a petrol-driven 3hp Donkey Engine. John Clemons does the pulping, the crushed apples fall into another trough, and from this trough is taken to the press. The method of pulping is simple - John has a pole about three-to-four feet in length, on one end a flat wooden head. All that he does is push the apples against the revolving drum, a loud crunch as the apples are pressed against the drum. Anything that would hold apples was pressed into use, corn sacks on loan from a Miller, to name one Adkins and Thomas, on loan simply guaranteed the Miller got the corn when it was thrashed. Keith Bennett filled the buckets from the trough into buckets, and Geoffrey Clifton bucketed it away to the press, where the pulped apples were placed onto coconut matting sheets about four feet square. When filled, they were called Cheeses and put carefully under the press, a number of these cheeses were put under the press before any juice was squeezed out. Geoffrey Clifton, a male nurse at the Ellen Badger Hospital, John Clemons a blacksmith, and Albert Batchelor retired pensioner previously served full-time with the Royal Gloucestershire Regiment, served in Hong Kong, Turkey, and finally in Germany 1914/18 War. They squared the cheeses, then Geoffrey and Tom Shepard, farmer of Sutton-under-Brailes, began to turn the press. Juice ran freely into another trough, from which it was taken in buckets to where the barrels stood waiting to be filled with apple juice. Thousands of gallons had been pressed from crushed apples during its lifetime. At present it is housed safely in retirement until someone requires a few gallons of cider. Then the wraps are taken off, and the process as described begins again.

You can see the apple juice pouring into the trough as pressure increases and then long poles are used to give extra leverage so that the final drops of juice can be pressed from the cheeses.

Keith Bennett, a farm student, waits with a full bucket of juice, waiting for Ted Shepard to empty the bucket he has into the barrel. After Ted and Tom Shepard's quota of apples have been pulped and pressed, the apple juice safely in the barrels, it is time for a break and a well-earned drink. Note the HORN GLASSES they are drinking from. Not the freshly-pulped juice I might add, but something a little stronger, for Mr Alan Goody, ex-Wing Squadron Leader RAF Retired, Landlord of The George Hotel, was also having a few apples pulped, and more than likely he had brought along a drop of Hooky Bitter.

Cyder could be turned into quite a potent, but nice drink by those who wanted to do the following, some put Legs of Mutton into the barrel or sultanas, as many pounds as you liked, depending on the size of your barrel, raisins, oranges, or several gallons of black treacle, but cider fed in this way. I know someone who fed his cider with all four of the last five mentioned. This, after 12 months, had to be treated with respect, no pint mugs, wine glasses a sensible way.

The team enjoying the drink are from left to right Tom Shepard, Alan Goody, Keith Bennett, John Clemons, Geoffrey Clifton, and Albert Batchelor. Mr Ted Shepard missing - he may have been a non-drinking man.

HARVEST TIME on Aitchill Farm, Brailes. The photograph shows William and Jack Dyke, farmers, Albion Alexander, cyder jar in hand, and William Warmington. The cyder jar was what cyder making is all about. Cyder taken into the fields during haymaking and harvest, and this keeps the workers happy and refreshed throughout a hot summer's day. When the thrashing drum arrives, to thrash out the stacked corn, cyder appears in the farmyard in jugs. If it is a cold winter's day, the farmer's wife or the farmer himself, will bring out a saucepan filled with hot cyder he has warmed over the kitchen fire. This is what cyder making is all about, never let the fruit rot away, gather it and make it into cyder, providing liquid refreshment when it was most needed.

BRAILES FLOWER SHOW was brought into life in 1943, War Weapons Week. How could we raise money for the War Effort. A flower show was suggested and agreed to. A committee was formed - Chairman Mr Percy Manley, Committee Harold Neal, Frank Miller, Len Horton, Gerald and Mrs Cotterill, Edwin Claydon, and others. The day arrived and so did the rain. It fell all day. At opening time Len Horton with overcoat on and sitting under an umbrella was taking money from people intent on making the day a success.

The flower show and sports, followed by a dance in the marquee was held in Burnt Orchard by the courtesy of Hubert Green. The opening ceremony was over in minutes, and everyone dived for shelter in the marquee. The band had been allocated one corner of the marquee and there it stood, all 15 or so members left after so many had been called to serve their country in the war against Germany. Between breaks in the band's playing, members could have a wander round to look at the exhibits, and so the afternoon went on. True to form at about 6.00 pm when the sports were scheduled to start, the rain ceased as if someone had turned a tap off. Sports began and ended without a spot of rain and, when the prize winners were hearing their names shouted out, it was almost time for the dance to begin. All that remained to do was get the trestles down and make room for the dancers. Still no rain, and at midnight, when the dance ended, it was still fine. At band practice the following Tuesday night the band members had a discussion about the future of the band, for with only a handful of players and a few from other villages, there was no possibility of finding enough players and so all instruments were handed in. Some players retained their instruments, and the band stopped playing until after the war. Then see who turned up to restart it.

In 1993 it was Brailes Flower Show's 50th Anniversary. Since 1943 there had been an annual holding of the Flower Show since it's initial beginning. It became an annual re-union for many, for years, evacuees, visitors who during the first few year after the war had country holidays, until the beaches had been cleared of land mines and barbed wire entanglements. School friends who had left in search of work returned annually.

Today, sadly, this is not the case for the years have taken their toll. Guest houses cropped up all around the village and did a roaring trade until seaside resorts were open for trade. The two local taverns enjoyed many, many good old-fashioned sing songs, the only places for an enjoyable evening. True dances were arranged during these holiday periods, and as usual good crowds were guaranteed at the show. Tony Weston, Shipston's Town Crier, was in attendance in 1988, held on 5th August that year. The photograph allows us to see him talking to five-year-old Thomas Edmunds, Daniel Edmunds who was six-years-old, with Tony's hand bell, and four-year-old John Argule.

Moving on to 1993, the 50th Anniversary, we have the cutting of the anniversary cake. Had Mr Percy Manley been alive, without doubt he would have had the honour of cutting it, but in his place we saw his son, William, preparing to do the honour. A fitting person, for he had attended virtually every show over the years and also been an exhibitor.

In 1993 we saw Tony Weston's son standing behind William Manley as he cut the cake. Ralph Welch has told me numerous stories, for he was sent out early on show day to bring in exhibitors and their exhibits to the showground. At Tredington Ralph had thought he had loaded the van ready for departure. "Is that it?" he asked the exhibitor, "not quite" he replied, "we will hang on for a couple of minutes". Just at that time the Stratford Blue Bus pulled up, and the conductor handed this competitor a parcel. He returned to the van and said, "we can go now young man". But the one I like most is this - Two non-gardeners of Brailes took their wives for a spin around the Cotswolds and stopped in one village where they saw a massive marrow. Five days later at Brailes Flower Show this massive marrow was in the heavy marrow class and won first prize. They are no longer with us, and Brailes the loser at their departure.

But providing this type of spirit still exists, but look at the allotments and gardens, I do have my doubts. And the liquidation of Brailes Brass Band, who played annually at this event, having begun its career in 1934, and at that time for Armistice Sunday, practiced marching to the tune ABIDE WITH ME set to march time in CARRY HAY, needs a miracle, I imagine, to see a band play at the Brailes Flower Show.

The History of Brailes Brass Band goes back to 1911, and the photograph I have of this band was taken as they played outside Miss Gurney's home at Lower Brailes, dressed in the discarded tunics of Sibford Band, no longer in existence. Those known at the time were William Warmington solo cornet and bandmaster, Danny Hemmings, Leonard Box, Raymond Box, Harry Woodward, and Alfred Cummings.

Miss Gurney must have thought they were in need of some better uniforms and she purchased a completely new set and gave them to the local band, who in 1911, the same year that they had played outside her home, they reappeared resplendent in their new uniforms and played again as a thank you to the lady, who was well-known for many small charitable acts during her lifetime. Those known at the time were William Warmington bandmaster, Raymond Box, Leonard Box, Owen Warmington son of William, and Harry Woodward, others unknown.

Above - Brailes Band outside Miss Gurney's home in 1911.
Below - Brailes Band playing outside Manor Farmhouse in 1912. Members were Danny Hemmings, Thomas Hawtin, Alfred Cummings, Harry Gregory, William Warmington, and Frank Bryan, who also played with the POP and GLORY BOYS, Brailes Temperance Band, who practised in the Methodist School Room on College Green. The year 1912.

Brailes, Sutton, and Cherington Brass Band. At the rear are Cecil Bryan, Cyril Bartlett, Tom Hawtin, Harry Box, George Print, William Warmington, Bert Print, Dasher Davis. Front - Owen Warmington, Dan Hibberd, others unknown. Below - Brailes Band at Little Compton Flower Show.

Brailes after being without a Band for many years, was reformed in 1934 after a General Meeting was held in the Institute. No instruments, except for ones personally owned or belonging to another band. In response to the meeting, a committee was formed, and a collection was made, members going round the village. Enough money was collected to purchase some instruments that were on offer at Hornton. Shortly after its first practice session, a matter of about six weeks, the band was asked to play at the Church Fete. It was task impossible, but nonetheless Frank Webb, the bandmaster, decided to do it. I helped him write in the fingering for some of the young players, and on the day the band got through its first engagement with just a few wrong notes played. 1937/38 Brailes Band went to play at Ilmington Flower Show. The band members were Bert Smith, Tom Smith, Dennis Jefferies, Charles Webb, Pop Turnell, Alfred Woodward, Ben Webb, Vincent Bryan, Edwin Bryan, F V Webb bandmaster, and an old Brailes bandsman went for the ride, Harry Woodward. The band pictured below.

Master Gavin Clemons began his musical career with Brailes Brass Band. After he left school he was accepted by the ROYAL MARINE SCHOOL OF MUSIC and, since joining, he has passed with top honours on four different types of instruments and travelled all over the world with THE ROYAL MARINE BAND, appearing on television and has a number of recordings of his solo performances at a number of concerts. He comes from a musical family, David, his father, was solo cornet player in Brailes Band and played solo cornet in Shipston-on-Stour Silver Band. His grandfather at the age of 14 years of age chose the Double BB Bass as the instrument he wanted to play. From 14 years of age he continued to play the Double BB into the 1990's. His only break was during the 1939/45 war when he served with the Warwickshire Yeomanry, having put his age on when joining at Honington Hall in 1937. His great-grandfather was solo tenor horn in the Melton Mowbray Silver Band for almost all his life, only leaving that band on his retirement and a move to Brailes, where he continued playing until the Band became redundant. With such a background, no wonder Gavin made it to the top.

Above - Brailes Brass Band outside St George's Church 1950's/60's. At the rear are Harry Webb, Dennis Jefferies, UK, UK, Gordon Pearce. In the front - John Clemons, Peter Daglish, UK, Pop Slater, Peter Crook, Colin Locke, UK, Dennis Abbotts, Charlie Pearce, young boy in front UK. Bottom - John Clemons on right, a guest player with Shipston-on-Stour Prize Silver Band.

Top - Melton Mowbray Town Silver Prize Band. Pop Slater solo tenor horn, fourth from left, centre row. Below - Brailes Silver Band preparing to entertain the people attending the WINDERTON OPEN DAY in August 1987. Player in the grey suit with signpost behind him is the late Sparks Hancock solo cornet in Shutford Band, also made many appearances with the Brailes Band since 1936/7.

The Brailes House of today is not the original. A farmhouse has been suggested, but I imagine from the long list of tenants who rented the Manor of Brayles, it was most likely a mansion of some size and more than likely the present manor house was a new house built in similar lines to its original. In the 52ⁿᵈ year of Will Manduit, Earl of Warwick, Will de Beauchamp took possession, holding in demesn three carucates and a park of 33 acres and a warren of conies. A carucate is as much land as a single team of Oxen can plough in one season. So a park was already established in Brailes and so that rules out Willington and Sheldon.

The Royal Manor of Brayles was 5520 acres in 1070. Tanworth was part of the Manor of Brayles and in that year the Parish of Brayles yielded the King £55 and 20 packhorse loads of salt in payment for timber sold from Tanworth to the Salt Works at Droitwich.

In 1868 Tanworth was no longer a part of the Manor of Brailes, for in that year it was 3,271 acres, and Brailes House would have been the one shown in the top photograph on page 168. Edward Ralph Charles Sheldon, born 2ⁿᵈ March 1782, took possession of Brailes House Estate. He married Marcella, the only daughter of Thomas Meredith Winstanley of Lissen Hall, Co Dublin. They had eight children, but only three survived, and in 1823 there were just a son and a daughter living, the son, Henry James Sheldon, and his sister, Isabel Calmady. Edward Sheldon was a staunch supporter of the Church. He became Church Warden and also a Major with the Warwickshire Militia, Deputy Lieutenant of Warwick, Justice of the Peace, and became the Member of Parliament for South Warwickshire in 1835. His death in June 1836 aged 54 years left his only son, H J Sheldon, owner of the whole of Brailes House Estate. After the death of H J Sheldon in 1902 the estate was sold. Miss Nelson was the purchaser. After her death in 1920 the whole of the Brailes Estate was sold off to private buyers or sitting tenants. No longer a Royal Manor or a Town. Brailes House had the south wing pulled down by the new owner, making the house smaller and easier to sell, but instead, after a timber merchant had purchased and felled all the timber, the builders took over, and all the outhouses were converted into flats and small houses.

— BRAILES HOUSE —

Brailes House as it used to be will completely disappear if the plans to build on the site of the old garden are passed. The bricks surrounding the garden will no doubt be used to build the new houses etc. for there are a few thousand bricks in the massive walls surrounding it. Likewise, the Twin Carp Ponds in the Old Rookery plus the Old Rookery with its massive trees have also disappeared.

Above - The old wooden bridge.

Below - For comparison is the New Bridge erected by the Local Council. The latter bridge should last for years. The old wooden one served its purpose well, for I must have walked along it scores of times in my school days. I still insist that the number of stones, counting the ones running down to the bridge in to Church Leasow five in number, made it with footstones running from the bridge, 109 steps.

Above - This is what the locals call the Ninety-nine steps, a Celtic trackway, which runs through to Bredon Hill. It is close to Castle Hill, a Celtic Fortification and a lookout point, for track ways run on either side of it. The cleft on the north side was most likely where the soil was dug to make what is obviously a man-made defence. Below - The old wooden bridge, which allowed anyone to cross the stream dry-footed.

In 1968, by kind permission of Mr Basil Taylor, the Sixth Form Boys from Shipston High School with their teacher, Mr Geoffrey Lewis, began an exploratory dig in the barn round on Springfield Farm and continued until 1971. Mr Lewis gave up about 18 months later, but Mr Barry Blount, of Shipston-on-Stour, a teacher at Stratford-upon-Avon, continued together with Mr Crayton Walker of Snitterfield. Barry kept a record of all finds, but from what I have found out and have in most cases seen, the accounts were bound to provide a false impression. I have given quite a good account in my book, Memories of Brailes, on this site, and I know what I have written in that book is true.

I firmly believe that Leonardine was the HAMLET of CHELMSCOT, depopulated by William Willington, and the only conclusive evidence of Roman occupation is in the field above Leonardine, that is the field named Black Pits. This is where a Roman Foundry was sited, some evidence, mostly nails, were found, but nothing very conclusive. I believe there was a Romano Site in what is now known as Orchard Close, for when the top soil was being taken away and tipped along the side of Holloway Lane, some decorative tiles were unearthed and quickly thrown onto the lorry and taken away. Builders did not want their development of this area halted.

An unknown school boy in Trench Two. I believe a few boys continued working with Barry Blount, present whereabouts unknown. The Bridge and Willow Tree are close to the site they were excavating. Roman Broaches and Rings I have seen were found closer to the village. A broach and a ring were found in THE LAPSTONE by Mr Phillip Suffolk and, just prior to his illness, he still had them at Rectory Farmhouse.

If we go north from the Bridge into The Barn Ground on Springfield Farm, you won't see this bridge anymore, for years after my grandfather, T H Woodward, built it, it stood the test of time as cart and wagon went over it, carrying corn to the Water Mill in The Barn Ground for grinding into flour. The children standing beneath were Mrs M Taylor's grandchildren. It was when spade lugged tractors began going over the bridge, that the bricks were loosened and finally the bridge collapsed into the stream below THE TIN MILL stood on the banks of the stream in the Barn Ground on Springfield Farm, owned by Tat Taylor, who had the firm of Henry and Frank Atwood, and their skilled workforce built the Mill. Thomas Henry Woodward Stonemason, built the Bridge on the south side of it, allowing cart and wagon loads of corn to cross the stream from the Third Leasow. The fields which run from the north side of St George's Church are named the first, second, and third Leasows, one and two are separated by a wire fence, for it is really one large field. He also built the sluice gate. He did the brick work, and most likely the timber work was done by John Claydon, carpenter. From the sluice gate the stream ran in almost a perfect 'S' bend. Photographs have provided the artist of this impression with an almost perfect background scene of what is really there. By the 1930's, although the tin-clad building was still intact, the floor boards were gone. So were the Mill Stones, but beneath the timbers which used to carry the floor boards, you could still see almost all of the shafting. The large wheel, which was directly behind the large undershoot Mill Wheel is still in its original position, and I suspect that some more shafting may still be there.

I can remember the times during the birds nesting season when Tom Boyce, John Clemons, Charlie Cuthbert, Henry Warmington, Marshall Green, and myself scouring the hedgerows, taking out the occasional eggs, but leaving enough in the nests so the young could be hatched out, having grabbed a dry crust of bread from the pantry, we ended up at the tin mill. We had tins and bricks in which we lit a fire, the tins were filled with water from the brook, and when they were cooked, out they came spread on to the bread and butter, a pinch of salt. We had not forgotten that and we thoroughly enjoyed the egg sandwiches. A bonus if we found Moor Hen, Partridge, or Pheasants eggs for they really made a meal. A picture of before and after in ones mind, but we never had the money like the large amounts in circulation today. Not much left for luxuries out of 26s to 30s a week, for a 44-hour week, unless there was some overtime to be worked. The JUST WILLIAM gang of Brailes.

This Mill Wheel does not appear to have deteriorated over the past 70-odd years, and I do not think that it is just this wheel. I am certain from what I saw as a school boy that more of the drive shafts are there to be uncovered and perhaps to have them housed as a reminder to future generations how water power was used extensively in the past.

How the Mill Site looked about ten years ago, when I took these two photographs. The Willow tree had been topped, and the briars and thorn bushes cut down to ground level. The end of an era. We may never see the likes again. The high banks, in some areas manmade, upstream shows how the water had the power to drive the mill, but look at the width of the stream, how it brought the water into a straight line.

Tin Mill Artists Impression.
This is how the tin mill possibly looked.

After leaving the Tin Mill site we walked back to what became known as Jack Crook's Lane. As we walked down towards the High Street we passed a block of red brick buildings. They were a pig sty, wood hovel, slaughter house, two starving pens, a three-stall stable, trap house with loft over, and a yard at the rear of these buildings.

In 1897 Alfred Lyne was butcher, working at these premises, together with his wife, Mary. They had a daughter named Anne. She married Mr Jack Crook, and they had two children, a son Robert, and a daughter Joan. Robert went into business, at first selling radios and then televisions when that became the in thing. Robert's shop was in the small building below the brick buildings. You can see the window above Wall Top height.

Joseph Green was slaughterman for Jack Crook. One day Marshall, his son, had to take a message to his father, and I went with him. Joe showed us how he had killed the beast he had hanging from ceiling height, which he had begun to skin, killed with a poleaxe in those days. After he had removed the skin it was hung out to dry and, when that was completed, the skin or skins would be sent on Harold Matthews's horse-drawn carrier cart to the Tannery in Stratford-upon-Avon. He showed us the poleaxe, an iron ball with a spike protruding from it, and having a handle to it about three feet in length. This Joe would swing quite quickly, spike pointing at the beast's head, and then on impact the spike pieced through the beast's skull, penetrating into the brain.

Passing these buildings we can see when we get into the High Street that Miss Joan Crook, who ran the family business until her retirement, had let the shop, and it is now a hairdresser's salon. Having spoken at some length about the businesses we see in High Street, we continue on down to THE BRIDGE. No one seems to know when it was built, but certainly well over 100 years. The Bridge Cottages have quite interesting history.

According to J Harvey Bloom, NANCE A was the witch of Brailes and she lived with her deformed child in one of the cottages. She could and did change herself into a cat or a hare. At such times she disappeared into the night and on one occasion a man was shooting on Gillettes Hill. Suddenly a hare ran past him; he shot at it, but it disappeared from view. Next morning Nance A came out of her cottage with her arm in a sling. She could get young girls to walk across the ceiling, without falling. If any woman upset her, she could stop the oven door from opening when they were cooking and not let it open until the meal was burnt to a cinder. It was all over by the 1920's, but her fame lived on. Stephen Stayley's widow lived in One Bridge Cottage, A Pickering in the other. Stephen was a plumber, and his sign can still be seen above the arches between the Old Police Station and the one the opposite side.

Above - How Bridge Cottages look today. Sold by Mr Derick Mumford, who has had a bungalow built on the garden that went with the cottages.

Across the road can tell a few stories. Originally it was THE BRAILES LOCK-UP 1864. I still have to find out if the Cell is still there or has been pulled down, which would have taken some time and energy. Henry James Sheldon's gamekeeper, named DITTON, was locked up in that cell, no window, just a small iron grill about eight inches round and set into a three-to-four inch solid oak door. It had two iron bars. Once a prisoner was inside, no way could he get out until let out, for the two iron bars slotted into two iron brackets and to make doubly sure no-one could let him out it had a massive padlock. Once in position and the key turned, it would have taken a tank to break the door down. Ditton had shot Henry Clifton on a public footpath on Grove End Farm. Henry died from the shotgun wounds. Angry villagers clambered onto the roof of the lock up, trying to get at Ditton, but to no avail. Next day he was taken to Warwick Gaol, where he was to stand trial. Ditton's brother walked to and from Warwick every day to see if notice of his brother's trial was to take place, but it never happened, for Ditton died in Warwick Gaol before he was tried.

Mrs Betty Smith found the latter part of this story when doing some research work and told me this story. Thank you Betty.

Happier memories about this house can be told, for during my school days Mr Harry Biddle was the owner of the garage and can be seen outside talking to some unknown motorcyclist riding a combination with his wife, Mrs Biddle, an onlooker. Also two school boys, one appears more interested than the other. Mrs Biddle gave piano tuition to anyone who was interested in that particular musical instrument, while Harry also sold Petrol and had two cars, which he did taxi work with. CANON PORTER lived at Brailes Vicarage and did relief preaching. One Sunday he was to preach at Oxhill morning service and again for Evensong. Brailes to Oxhill via Whatcote, a gated road, and a road filled with potholes. He asked me if I would go with them to open the gates, for which he would pay me One Shilling. He picked up Canon Porter and he got in the front while I clambered into the Dickie Seat. Stop, start, clamber in and out of the Dickie Seat. In between Harry hit pot hole after pot hole, each time I was almost thrown out of the Dickie Seat, nothing to hold onto. On the return journey I sat in the front seat, that was not too bad, but by 6.30 pm, a dark, cold night, I failed to turn up for the second edition of that journey. How Harry got on I do not know, for he never offered me sixpence for the morning journey, and I did not ask him for it. The worst journey of my life.

Above - The earliest view I have seen of the BRIDGE taken before the Poplar Tree was planted and about the time the house on the right was the Police Station. I can only guess who the three ladies are - I would imagine by their dress that they may have come down to Jeffs Close from the nearby Brailes House at the times the Sheldons were living there 1864/1897, about the time the estate was being sold. A possible clue it might have been Miss Nelson viewing what was to be sold.

Where has the Church gone?